EVEN JESUS NEEDED MONEY

A Conversation Guide On Money And Stewardship

By

Dennis R. Maynard, D. Min.

DIONYSUS PUBLICATIONS

Dionysus Publications
www.Episkopols.com
49 Via Del Rossi
Rancho Mirage, California 92270

Email: Episkopols@aol.com

Telephone: 760.324.8589

ISBN:1543021689

Dionysus Publications

Books For Clergy And The People They Serve.
www.Episkopols.com

*Surveys indicate that Americans find it more difficult to discuss money with the people in their lives than sex, politics, or religion. Yet money remains one of the primary reasons for marital and family breakdown. Most every pastor and Church leader routinely restricts conversation about money to the annual stewardship drive. Even then, they often sound apologetic.

What if you had a resource that could help you factually discuss money and charitable giving with your spouse, children, church board, and parish members? This book could help you do so without fear, embarrassment, or anxiety. The following pages just could be the very vehicle you can use to have a frank and honest conversation about money with the people in your life.

*This is the only reference footnote in this book. It's just too easy to go to the modern library, the Internet, to research and read in more detail the studies referenced on the following pages.

TABLE OF CONTENTS

FOR SPECIAL OFFERS
AND
VOLUME DISCOUNTS,
ORDER DOCTOR MAYNARD'S BOOKS
AT:

www.Episkopols.com

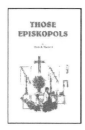

Those Episkopols

Forgive & Get Your Life Back

The Magnolia Series (9 Books)

When Sheep Attack

Preventing A Sheep Attack

Healing For Pastors and People Following A Sheep Attack

FORWARD

"It is not good for a person to have desire
and be without knowledge
(Proverbs 19:2)."

Let's talk about money! That one suggestion has the power to stir up both anxiety and dread in most any relationship. Too often, the subject of money is not even broached until there is absolutely no other alternative. The topic of money is invariably emotion-driven and can spark the most heated of arguments.

Spouses often avoid the conversation until it's too late and the marriage is on the verge of collapse. Children seldom want to hear the words *budget, we can't afford it,* or *it's too expensive.*

If a spender happens to be married to a saver, a mix that happens more often than I even thought possible, the tension in the relationship can drive one or the other to the breaking point. The relationship becomes gangrenous when the spender repeatedly runs up debt and then presents it to the saver to pay for them. Such behavior has sent more than one saver running for the door.

Often, divorced or widowed couples in second marriages have failed to draw clear lines between yours, mine, and ours. Such an understanding needs to be set up in a trust or at the very least in another written agreement. Failure to do so will inevitably lead to conflict with the children as major players.

In our current world both spouses are often employed outside the home. Unless there is a clear conversation held in advance another destructive scenario develops. The one spouse believes the money they earn belongs to them, but they also believe the money the other spouse earns belongs to them as well. It's the classic version of what's mine is mine and what's yours is mine also. The resentment built up over time can be monumental and can become a driving force in a divorce.

Inheritances, while appearing to be a blessing, can also destroy a relationship. If the spouse receiving the inheritance in the marriage does not consider it to be a marital asset, then that can leave the other spouse feeling used. In this dynamic, the one spouse is supposed to continue to provide for the household from their earned income. The other spouse spends the windfall as they choose. It is as though their marital partner doesn't even exist. This dynamic has been described as leaving the one partner feeling like the other got the goldmine while they got the shaft.

Even in the Church, the topic of money is approached with caution. As necessary as it is to have an annual pledge drive, it will be a source of irritation for some members of the congregation. The familiar statement, *All they do is talk about money down at that church,* was coined for just such a purpose.

Over my four decades of pastoral ministry, I yearned for a deeper conversation about money with my congregations. My pastoral ministry with the various members of the parish informed that desire. I knew that many of them were having financial difficulties. Some were suffering because of job loss or extraordinary medical bills. These events were beyond their control.

My primary pastoral concern was for those folks burdened by self-inflicted financial wounds. Their money was already stretched too thin even before they exacerbated their money problems. I knew first-hand that many of their marriages were feeling the strain of poor money management. I yearned for a guide that I could give them so that in the privacy of their homes they could have an insightful and honest conversation about money from a Christian perspective.

I wanted to have the same dialogue with the leadership of the parish. Too often those elected to administer the financial resources of the parish knew little about money management or stewardship. All the

9

above listed needs are the motivating force that has led to the writing of this book.

My hope is that this book will be a resource to stimulate conversation about money management and its stewardship. It will offer some informative and provocative thoughts about money and charitable giving. It can be utilized in small groups. Youth leaders may find it a valuable resource. Pastors could easily utilize it in premarital and marital counseling. The following pages contain critical information for stewardship committees and parish governing boards. A good starting place might be to review this book with our own spouse and children.

A new stewardship campaign will not be presented. Nor will a campaign strategy or a new campaign slogan be recommended. The following pages are dedicated to stimulating conversation about money and being faithful stewards of it. The insights offered are spiritual lessons. Teaching faithful Christians to incorporate the stewardship of money into their spiritual journey is an ongoing challenge for every pastor. Clergy and congregational governing boards are not just confronted with the task of raising a budget each year. Our ministry is to teach the people in our care how to develop a spiritually healthy concept of money. If we are faithful to that task, the annual budget just may take care of itself.

So, let's talk about money. It is my hope that this spiritual guide will allow you and the people in your life to do so without anxiety or dread. My prayer is that it will help you do so factually, openly, and with good humor.

Dennis Maynard, D. Min.
Rancho Mirage, California

Questions To Stimulate Conversation

Do you find it difficult to talk about money management with your spouse? Your children? Is it a volatile subject? Why or why not?

Have you ever volunteered to lead the stewardship campaign for your parish? What surprised you? What disappointed you? What did you learn?

Have you participated in a stewardship campaign that met or exceeded its goal? In your opinion, what factors contributed to its success?

ACKNOWLEDGEMENT

As this book is being finalized, I am the resident priest at Saint Jude Episcopal Church in Ocean View, Hawaii. This is one of the most remarkable congregations I've ever served. It is located in one of the poorest sections of the United States. Some beautiful Hawaiian style houses surround the mission. Tents and plywood shelters that serve as homes for other residents are also present.

The Sunday attendance at Saint Jude averages forty to sixty people. Last year forty-three thousand people utilized the building. Two other congregations also worship in the church on Sundays. Saint Jude reaches out to the surrounding community by offering free showers and hot meals on Saturdays. Multiple self-help addiction groups meet in the building most every day. They host the local food bank, clothing distribution, and senior nutrition three days a week.

Beyond these extensive outreach ministries, the congregation is one of the most loving and accepting I've ever experienced. The worship services are vibrant and inspiring. At the Aloha Hour following the service, retired professionals are seated next to tent people, chatting and sharing a meal. The people of Saint Jude are a living example of the insights I strive to impart in this book.

stjudeshawaii.org

This book is dedicated to my parents,
Hue Roy and Roxie Ola Maynard.

*They loved me so much that
they did not give me everything I wanted.*

CHAPTER ONE

CAN YOU SURVIVE WITHOUT MONEY?

"Whatever you do, work at it with all your heart as though you are working for the Lord (Colossians 3:23)."

Country singer Chris Janson sings,

I know everybody says
Money can't buy happiness
Yeah, and I know what they say,
Money can't buy everything
Well, maybe so,
But it could buy me a boat.

Money is a necessary evil. That is a familiar expression. Like it or not, money is a necessity. It is an essential tool for survival. It has no intrinsic value of its own. Money is neither good nor evil. Money is a medium of exchange. Its value is determined by how we use it.

There are those that want to use money to elevate their status in life. They believe money can purchase prestige. Others want to use it to buy power and control. They believe they can use their money to intimidate others. They believe they can buy deference with it. For others, money is a symbol of their success and a mark of their intelligence, genius, or creativity. If given the opportunity, they would happily attach their financial statement to their social page. Still others, like Ebenezer Scrooge, simply want to stockpile money. They want to accumulate it. They don't intend to spend it, help anyone, or exchange it for any material object beyond the basic necessities. Others deceive themselves into thinking money can buy happiness.

Money is required in order to buy food, shelter, and clothing. Money is necessary. The necessities of life require that we earn money. Jesus and his disciples needed to spend money. They used money. They had a treasury and a treasurer.

According to one source, the Bible makes 2,000 references to money. The Bible has only 500 verses on prayer. The Gospels speak of money 288 times. The scriptural teachings regarding money desperately need to be reinforced. I recently read that the average American is precisely three weeks from bankruptcy. A recent news story reported that sixty-four percent of Americans don't even have one thousand dollars set aside in savings should they need it for an emergency. Absent significant savings and investments, burdened with extraordinary debt and a standard of living that exceeds income, we are a people totally dependent on the next paycheck.

Some say money problems are now the number one reason for marital difficulty. Even with two-income families, the marital breakdown is primarily financial. Spousal desertion and acts of suicide because of financial strain are beginning to escalate to proportions closely resembling those of the Great Depression.

As I write this, far too many Americans are feeling the effects of an economy that has not provided them the opportunities they need. Many authorities argue the monthly numbers on employment reported by our government are not accurate and are actually deceptive. Some argue that the unreported numbers are staggering. They believe that millions of Americans have given up looking for a full-time job. These individuals are not included in the government's statistics.

Only 47% of us are working at full-time jobs while the available number of part-time jobs has soared to over twenty-eight million. Unemployed adults eagerly seek after jobs that would have normally been introductory level positions for teenagers. Far too many adults work at two or more part-time jobs to provide for their families and themselves. But these jobs pay less, have diminished to non-existent benefits, and less job security. Add to this the fact that now one in seven

Americans receive food stamps in order to feed their families. On the other hand, some economists project that within just a few years, the top one percent of Americans will hold more wealth than the other ninety-nine percent of us combined.

Examining the spiritual implications of money will not increase our monetary wealth one penny. These chapters are not intended to reveal the secrets that are supposed to help us *get rich*. There is a greater insight I want to bring to the light. It is contained in a haunting refrain penned by Saint Paul to the congregation in Philipi. *"I have learned the secret of being content in any and every situation."* He introduced that sentence with this one. *"I know what it is to be in need, and I know what it is to have plenty.... whether well fed or hungry, whether living in plenty or want* (Philippians 4:12-13).*"*

Just what is that secret? In particular, what was the secret that Saint Paul had learned when it came to money and material possessions? The Blessed Apostle prefaced those words with these that echo the Sermon on the Mount. *"Do not be anxious about anything, but in every situation, by prayer and petition, with thanksgiving, present your requests to God. And the peace of God, which transcends all understanding, will guard your hearts and your minds in Christ Jesus* (Philippians 4:5-7).*"*

When we examine the material aspects of this world with a spiritual lens, we will see them in a new way. When we bring God into our thinking about money, we will realize just how rich we already are.

Chris Janson is correct.

Money can't buy happiness.
But it could buy me a boat,
it could buy me a truck to pull it.

Questions To Stimulate Conversation

Draw a quick sketch of the happiest time in your life financially.

Then draw a quick sketch of the saddest time in your life financially.

Finally, draw a quick sketch of where you are right now in your life financially. Explain your sketches to the other members of the group.

CHAPTER TWO

HOW MUCH MONEY DO YOU NEED TO JUST GET BY?

"Whoever loves money never has enough; whoever loves wealth is never satisfied with their income (Ecclesiastes 5:10).*"*

The story is told that the elder Mister Rockefeller was once asked, "How much money is enough?" The multi-millionaire responded, "A little bit more than I have right now." It appears that there is some truth in that statement. Several years ago, Ernst and Young conducted a sample survey of affluent Americans. The average income of those surveyed was $194,000 dollars a year. The average net assets were $775,000 dollars. The survey concluded that forty percent of these folks did not feel financially secure. Twenty percent did not see themselves as financially well off. When asked about their priorities, the majority listed personal success first. Money was listed over family.

In a similar survey, *The Independent Sector* noted that households that gave two percent or more of their income to charity were not the affluent, but the poor. These studies raise the question – *do we possess our money or does our money possess us?*

The reports suggest that the more we have, the harder it is to loosen our grip on it.

I remember reading a study done by a group of university sociology students. They did a survey of people who stated that they earned a salary of $100,000 dollars or more a year. Given the worst-case scenario, the residents were asked just how much money they would need in a given year to simply get by. $50,000 dollars a year was the average response. In order to live comfortably on less, the residents reported that they would need at least $88,000 dollars a year. When asked what they would need to achieve all their dreams, they asserted that $250,000 dollars a year would be sufficient.

The students then went into an area of the city where they knew incomes were much lower. The average income was $35,000 dollars a year. The students asked the same questions. Here the residents responded that they could get by on $25,000 dollars a year. They would need $30,000 dollars to live comfortably, but if they had $50,000 dollars a year, they would be able to fulfill all their dreams.

The issue for every Christian is how much money is enough? As Christians, we condemn amassing wealth at the expense of others. Our fortunes should not be built on the backs of others. Such is contrary to the teachings of scripture and contrary to God's purpose for us.   Even if our livelihood is honorable, does there come the moment when we have amassed more than we need?

Japan has a rule of thumb that the top executive earns no more than ten times the corporation's entry level of pay.   Compare that to the American corporate CEO who earns sometimes a hundred times or more than that of the entry-level person.

How much is enough?   As long as money remains the benchmark for measuring status, power, prestige, and success, then the marketplace is highly competitive and enough will never be realized.   Do we need lots of money to justify our existence, to prove our worth, or to impress others? If so, we will always be in need of more.

Even if our livelihood is completely honorable,
does there come the moment for every Christian
when we have amassed more than we need?

I am not advocating desert asceticism or some pious form of Christian poverty. My suggestion is that Christians come to terms with the demonic possibilities of money.   I am advocating a *Theology of Enough.* To define our worth by the amount of money we can accumulate or the type of possessions we wear, own, drive, live in, is nothing less than demonic.

During my ministry, I was Rector of a parish-owned school. The governing board and vestry made a commitment to build a new middle school. A couple of physicians with children in the school presented me with the idea of asking the medical community to build and equip the science lab in the school. It was suggested that I ask each physician with an interest in the school to give $10,000 dollars for the science lab.

I will never forget one of the doctors that I visited with this request. His response was classic. He looked at me in dismay and exclaimed, "Do you think I'm made out of money? I only have six million dollars saved for my retirement!" A few days later I did receive a check from him for the science lab. It was for fifty dollars. Every Christian has to ask themselves this question, *how much is enough*?

I remember driving a friend through one of the exclusive neighborhoods in our city. We passed one of those mansions with ten bedrooms and twelve bathrooms on a five-acre lot. My friend shook her head, "I don't want to have the number of children it would take to justify owning a house that large."

A spiritual understanding of money is not just dependent on the amount we give to

Church and charity. It is dependent on how we earn it, otherwise spend it, and the value we place on it.

What we think the presence or absence of money says about the worth of a person is fundamentally a spiritual question. The line items in our checkbooks and on our credit card statements may be the clearest indicator of who and what we think is most important to us.

Questions To Stimulate Conversation

Given the worst-case scenario, how much would you have to earn each year to simply get by?

How much would you need to earn each year to fulfill all your dreams?

What makes you believe that fulfilling those dreams would add to your life? Explain.

CHAPTER THREE

ARE THE WEALTHY BLESSED OR JUST LUCKY?

"People who want to get rich fall into a trap and into foolish and harmful desires that plunge them into ruin and destruction. For the love of money is the root of all kinds of evil (I Timothy 6:9-10)".

It was one of those wedding invitations that anyone who was anyone in the parish community coveted. That meant they were included among the bride and groom's five hundred closest friends and family. That was the seating capacity of the parish church. Those guests were treated to a most opulent and visually pleasing wedding ceremony. The wedding reception included three hundred additional invitees. None of the private clubs in the city could host that many people, so several circus-sized tents were needed. They were linked together on the estate that the bride's parents called home.

White-gloved waiters in dinner jackets carrying silver trays filled with hors d'oeuvres greeted the eight hundred guests. Still other groomed waiters wearing crisp white shirts took drink orders. Every dinner table was adorned with extravagant floral displays. The gourmet meal was served with carefully chosen wines to go with each course.

After I had given the keys to my car to one of the red-coated valets in the candlelit circular driveway, my wife and I walked to the entrance. As we entered, I spotted one of my vestry members. I asked him, "Well, how is it?"

He chuckled, "It's just the kind of party God would throw if He had any money."

I have no doubt that the bride's parents could afford such a party. From what I'd learned about their inherited and earned wealth, I'm quite confident they could have paid for the entire event with cash on hand.

Too often, the untold story is just the opposite. An individual pretending to be wealthy did not, in fact, have the money to sustain their lifestyle. In order to maintain the pretense, they resorted to creative debt. The end result is always disastrous for those who are left behind.

I had been elected to the governing board of an academic institution. It was my first meeting. I was sitting next to an old friend who was finishing his last year on the board. Opposite us was a person that other members of the board had made a point of greeting when they entered the conference room. I didn't know the man, but from all the attention he was getting, I assumed the members thought he was very important.

That man dominated the meeting. He spoke to each item on the agenda. None of the other board members disagreed with his observations. A few nodded agreement each time, but I observed that most of the board members kept their eyes focused on the table. At one point, the chair of the board suggested that a specific decision would require a vote of the board. The man very angrily responded. "You just need to know that if the board votes in favor of this action, you will no longer have my support." The motion was defeated overwhelmingly.

During the break I asked my friend to tell me about the man. I confessed my confusion as to just why that one man seemed to be dominating the meeting. My friend informed me that the man was quite wealthy. The board was hoping that he would gift a large sum for the new building the institution was planning.

At the following meeting the man was not present. The chair informed us that the man had died. He also informed us that the institution had not been remembered in the man's final distribution of charitable gifts. It was later that I also learned that the man had only made the minimum contribution to the annual fund each year that was required of all board members.

It's a scene that I've seen played out over and over again in my life. Deference is paid to an individual, not because of their knowledge or expertise, but because of their wealth. The implication is that because of their large portfolio, they are more important. The conclusion is that their money lifts their status to that of royalty. They are of greater worth than those around them.

Contrast that experience with another. I was on the board of a charitable foundation. The chair of the board announced the death of a certain widow. She had been one of their most faithful kitchen volunteers for many years. The chair stated, "We never thought she was worth much, but folks, she left us over a million dollars!"

Too often a person's importance and success is equated with accumulating the material goods that money can buy. I recall seeing a bumper sticker that read - *At the end of the world, the one with the most toys wins*.

I like telling the story of the man who had just driven his brand new Rolls Royce automobile out of the showroom. He was smiling ear to ear. He came to a stoplight. A man driving a little Mazda Miata pulled up beside him. The driver motioned for the man in the Rolls Royce to roll down his window. The driver of the Mazda Miata asked, "Does that car have cruise control?"

The driver of the Rolls Royce responded indignantly, "It certainly does."

The Miata driver smiled, "So does my Miata. Do you have a navigation system in that car?"

The driver of the Rolls Royce gave the man an indignant, "Of course it does."

The driver of the Miata leered out of his window. "So does this Miata. Does that car have a queen size bed in it?"

"Of course not," shot the driver.

"Well, this Miata does." Just then the light changed and the Miata sped through the intersection. It was then that the Rolls Royce driver saw the vanity license plate on the Miata. It read simply, *I WIN*.

The driver of the Rolls Royce became furious. He drove his car back to the dealer. "I don't care how you do it, but I want a queen size bed put in the back of this car."

A few days later the dealer called and told the man they had done as he had instructed. His Rolls Royce now came fully equipped with a queen size bed. The man picked up his car and started down the freeway toward his home. He was feeling quite pleased with himself. It was then that he spotted the Miata. It was parked in a roadside park. He knew it was the same because of the vanity plate - *I WIN.*

The man pulled off the freeway and into the park. He pulled up behind the Miata. He knocked on the window of the Miata.

Eventually the driver of the Miata rolled down his window. "Yes, what can I do for you?"

The driver of the Rolls Royce pulled himself up so that he could look down his nose at the driver of the Miata, "I just want you to know that my Rolls Royce now has a queen size bed in it."

This time it was the driver of the Miata that became indignant, "You got me out of the shower just to tell me that?"

The logic of worldly success lies on a major fallacy,
the strange error that our happiness depends upon
the thoughts, opinions, and applause of others.
A weird life it is to be always living in someone else's imagination.
Thomas Merton

Here the teachings of Jesus need to be reinforced. All of God's children are of equal value. According to scripture, the burden falls on those of us who have been given any measure of wealth. In the eyes of God, the rich are at a disadvantage and not the poor.

Equally, we can argue that the worth and lasting value of the service we provide is not proportionate to the money we receive. The ability to extract enormous fees for our services just may be more compatible with a violation of one of the commandments than the true value of the service, *You shall not steal.*

When billionaire Howard Hughes died the question was asked, "How much did he leave?" People tried to estimate the amount of wealth he had left. I knew exactly how much he left. I knew to the penny. He left it all! There will come the day when each of us will leave it all. In the interim, we could still lose it all, or have it taken from us, or be deprived of its use. Will we be a lesser person separated from our wealth? Will we be less important? Will we believe our true worth as a person has decreased?

I read recently of a millionaire who, having reached an advanced aged, was in the process of giving away all of his money to charitable causes. That man's goal was to systematically time his giving in such a way that, on the day that he died, he would be broke. Clearly, here is a person who has learned to separate his value as a person from his money. If we were to ask him about his financial goals in life, I can hear him say, "I want to die a pauper".

It's an old cliché, but it's still filled with wisdom. On the ride to the cemetery, *no hearse has ever been followed by an armored truck.*

The first step toward financial freedom is to come to terms with this business of worth. Who we are - what we do - and the greater contribution we make are never to be confused with money. We must not ask for deference from others simply because we have more money. By the same token, we demean ourselves to defer to others precisely for the same reason.

Why do we settle for less and call it success?

In his book *Mere Christianity*, C. S. Lewis offered a proper perspective on money every Christian should hold. "One of the dangers of having a lot of money is that you may be quite satisfied with the kinds of happiness money can give and so fail to realize your need for God. If everything seems to come simply by signing checks, you may forget that you are at every moment totally dependent on God."

Questions To Stimulate Conversation

How is the following scriptural teaching relevant to the financial insights offered in this chapter?

"When Jesus noticed how the guests picked the places of honor at the table, he told them this parable: "When someone invites you to a wedding feast, do not take the place of honor, for a person more distinguished than you may have been invited. If so, the host who invited both of you will come and say to you, 'Give this person your seat.' Then, humiliated, you will have to take the least important place. But when you are invited, take the lowest place, so that when your host comes, he will say to you, 'Friend, move up to a better place.' Then you will be honored in the presence of all the other guests. For all those who exalt themselves will be humbled, and those who humble themselves will be exalted' (Luke 14:7-11).*"*

What are the symbols of success in your particular community? Have you ever been tempted by them? Why did you think you chose to yield or ignore these symbols of success?

Do you remember giving deference to another person simply because you believed they had more money than you? What were you feeling at the time?

Have you ever felt superior to another person simply because you have more money than you thought they did? What were you feeling at the time?

Has your church or organization ever *walked on eggshells* not to offend a wealthy member? If so, what were the results? Did that behavior help or hurt your parish or organization?

CHAPTER FOUR

HOW RICH DO YOU WANT TO BE?

"Those who want to get rich fall into temptation and many foolish desires. Flee from these things and pursue righteousness, faith, love, and gentleness
(I Timothy 6:9-11)."

I think it all begins when we are children and well meaning relatives ask us, "What do you want to be when you grow up?" The implication is that we must become something else. We must become something of greater worth. Too often, this message is then reinforced in most every high school commencement address. Many motivational speeches include the following phrase or some variation of the same, *Go from this place and make your mark on the world; become somebody!* The implication is that currently you are nobody. You must prove yourself so that you can become somebody.

But that's just the point. Our self-worth, our importance, our dignity, are not dependent on the amount of money we have or don't have. We must not confuse our self-worth with our net worth. Money is **not** a mirror of any person's worth! Sadly, the question is frequently phrased that way. "How much are they worth?" The size of their financial portfolio is by no means a reflection of the value of any person.

Our contemporary world defines a successful life with material symbols. There is the enormous salary, the year-end bonus, the corner office, the prestigious title on the door, designer labels, the big house behind the security gates, membership in exclusive clubs, the right automobile in the garage, and the ability to present one's daughter a royal wedding.

The trap that can destroy begins when we confuse our net worth with our self-worth.

Perhaps there is no event in the year that reinforces these empty symbols of success more than the annual *Walks of Narcissism* on the red carpet in Hollywood. Before these self-congratulatory award shows begin, interviewer after interviewer asks the critical question, "Who are you wearing?" The brand label of the dress and tuxedo are badges of success.

The irony for me is that the bejeweled often then challenge the rest of us to be more generous in our support of the poor, equal rights, or a host of other causes. Perhaps the final twist is the private jets and large limousines the Hollywood elite travel in following their speeches on global warming.

There just may be something to the expression that it doesn't take talent to spend other people's money. Or equally, *do as I say, not as I do*.

One of the most painful periods in my ministry occurred over a few short weeks one particular autumn. Four men in our parish community chose to end their own lives. Suicide, especially the suicide of a young person, invariably sends shockwaves through every community. I have stood at the graves of too many young people who have made the choice to end their own lives. I have looked into the grief-stricken faces of their spouses, children, parents, and friends. I have struggled to find words of comfort.

These particular four men shared a lot in common. They were all family men with children ranging from toddlers to teenagers. Each appeared to be happily married. On the surface it looked like they were enjoying a relative degree of success in life. They had homes in the *right neighborhoods*. They possessed automobiles that made success statements. Their children attended private schools. They belonged to exclusive clubs. Those who sat in shock at their funerals had a difficult time understanding why these men would end their own lives. By the world's standards, they had everything going their direction.

One man spread the pictures of his wife and children before him on a picnic table. He then put a pistol to his temple and pulled the trigger.

Another kissed his wife as she was preparing his dinner. He gave her a big hug and told her he was going upstairs to take a nap. The next thing she heard was the sound of the gun he had placed in his mouth.

Still another went into his garage. He put the garage door down and started his car engine. When his wife found him, he had her picture and that of his children in his shirt pocket.

And the fourth man went to his office on a Saturday morning. He told his family he needed to catch up on some work. The security guard heard the pistol go off. He discovered the man slumped over his desk.

Autopsies revealed each man was in excellent health. Physically, all four men could have looked forward to many more years of life. They had wives and children that loved them. They were gentlemen with status and respect in the community. The reasons for their suicides were revealed in the notes they left behind.

Each one felt like a failure. And each one, in the effort to maintain an image of success, had accumulated considerable business and personal debt. Each felt like they had let down those who loved them.

They believed they had no alternative but to take their own lives. In his suicide note, one suggested that all his paid up life insurance policies would allow his wife to increase her living standard beyond that which he would ever be able to provide for her.

Before judging these men too harshly, I would ask you to take another look at the success trap that surrounds all of us.

Sociologists conducted a survey of New Jersey teenagers. The sociologists asked the teens, "What do you believe you want to be when you grow up?" The vast majority of the teenagers responded, "wealthy, powerful, and famous". The teens equated wealth with worth.

The sociologist then went to a Hopi Indian reservation and asked the Hopi Indian teens the same question. "What do you want to be when you grow up?" The overwhelming response was "Hopi Indians". One cannot help but wonder who has a better sense of self-worth.

Finally I am coming to the conclusion
that my highest ambition
is to be what I already am.
Thomas Merton

Still we find ourselves asking about one another, "How much do you think they are worth?" Do we really believe that the person who has the ability to throw a ball through a basketball hoop is of more value than the classroom teacher? Of course not, but then compare the salary of the professional athlete with that of the educator. Or, it is even more astounding to discover that often the salary of the university athletic director substantially exceeds that of the university president.

The irony of experience over reason is manifold. If worth is to be determined by salary, then the rock musician contributes more to the welfare of humanity than any other occupation. Then again, we know that is not true. There is a commercial for a credit card company that lists the price of several items. It then describes a life experience. The experience, they say, is priceless.

Our self-worth has absolutely nothing to do with our net worth.

I was always grateful for the fact that, as a priest, I received a fixed salary that was determined by an independent board. If I had to invoice those I ministered to for services rendered, I would be at a loss. What does one charge for praying with a family while a loved one undergoes surgery? What do you charge for holding the hand of a dying person as they enter the life beyond? What do you charge for helping sinners, eaten up by their own guilt, to forgive themselves and get their lives back?

Some things in life are priceless.

Who we are, what we do, and the greater contribution we make, must never be confused with our ability to be compensated for it. Our worth is not dependent on the size of our paycheck or the bottom line of our financial statement. Our value transcends currency.

The most important things in life have no dollar value on them. The feel of my little grandchildren's hands in mine – what price tag would I put on that? Knowing that my sins are forgiven and that people love me in spite of myself – how much is that worth? How much for a warm embrace, a tender moment, a precious memory? Some things are beyond price. To put a price tag on the experience would cheapen it. The credit card company motto has it right. There are some things that are priceless.

I still remember holding the hand of a fellow priest and dear friend while he died. His wife and I were the only ones in the room with him. With broken voices and tear filled eyes, we prayed for him as he left us. Time and again she stated, "I don't know how I can thank you enough for being there with me." She soon received a bill from the hospital. They knew exactly how much to charge for being there. The same was true for her physician and the mortician. All knew their price. But what could I charge? Any price tag, even the most exorbitant, would be to cheapen such a sacred privilege.

I've walked through a lot of cemeteries. The predominant symbol on the gravestones is not the symbol of one's profession, the company logo, or even the balance on one's financial statement. The predominant symbol in death also needs to be the predominant symbol that marks our lives – the cross of Christ.

I believe that it was Saint Iraneus who introduced the practice of inviting the faithful to communion with the following words. He would present the consecrated bread and wine to the people and say – *"The mystery of yourselves is spread before you on this table. Come, eat, drink; become that which you already are."*

At our baptisms we each were sealed on our foreheads with the sign of the cross of Christ. We were marked with chrism and sealed as *Christ's own forever* (Book of Common Prayer page 308).

What do you want to be when you grow up? For the Christian, like the Hopi Indians, the answer is simple. We want to be who we are. We want to be a Christian, a child of God. We want to live into that which we already are. We are the body of Christ on earth. It is Christ that is within us. We are His ministers. Each Sunday the mystery of ourselves is spread before us on the altar. Let us eat, drink, and become that which we already are.

Questions To Stimulate Conversation

What are some experiences in your life that you would consider priceless?

What acts of kindness or ministry have you received from others that you would be unable to affix a dollar amount to?

What would change if we reinforced in our children an understanding that their self-worth is not dependent on achieving fortune, fame, or power?

Do the following words collide with the materialistic message of the world - *You are a member of a chosen race, a royal priesthood, and a holy nation* (I Peter 2:9). Why or why not?

What success messages did you receive as a child? What success messages do you continue to give yourself?

Have you ever felt like a failure? What role did money play in that feeling?

CHAPTER FIVE

ARE YOU WELL-HEELED?

"Keep your life free from the love of money, and be content with what you have (Hebrews 13:5)."

We sometimes refer to the wealthy as *well-heeled.* In some countries they are described as *prosperous.* Both terms are actually a reference to heavy-set people. The idea was that they were wealthy enough to afford all the food that they could eat. Their widened girth meant that should a famine occur, they would be able to literally live off their own fat. The common belief is that the well-heeled and the prosperous are secure.

I have even heard it argued that having excess money does make us more secure. I have pondered this notion and find it full of holes. What I have discovered is that the more money one has, the more security one needs.

We need safe deposit boxes and alarm systems protected with codes and digits. Security cameras we can monitor from our smart phones, gated communities with guards at the gate, and armed patrols are needed to secure our possessions. And if we become extremely wealthy, we will need especially designed automobiles and armed bodyguards to protect our loved ones and us.

Insurance policies are needed just in case we lose one of our valuables. Even more insurance policies are required just in case they are stolen, burned, or blown away. Insurance is needed when we die. And other insurance is needed just in case we live, but can't keep the money coming in.   All this begs the question: *At what point do we cease to own our possessions and they begin to own us?*

I've stood over the graves of the very wealthy and the very poor.   Some died because of an unforeseen accident, others disease, still others were fortunate enough to die of old age. One thing was certain - all did die. The absence or presence of money did not prevent death from making its appointed rounds. Again, I ask -- where is the security?

If the glossy covers on the supermarket magazines are to be believed, the wealthy always have friends and lovers. I would like to argue otherwise. If a person chooses a friend because the person is wealthy, that is not friendship at all, only a transaction. If I love another because they get to sit in the seat of honor in society, that is not love, just an arrangement.

If I should lose my money, would it mean that my friends and lovers could vanish just as easily? At least those that prostitute themselves are honest with themselves and their clients. *The boyfriend or girlfriend experience* can be purchased, but it will only last so long as the money does. Is there really a difference if wealth is the only glue binding the marriage or friendship? Where is the security in that?

"It will protect me in my old age."

"Fool!" Cries my soul.

Manifold are the stories in my personal diary of children, grandchildren, ill-scrupled guardians, and other heirs who studied at the feet of the prodigal son. They were unable to wait for their parents to die before gaining their inheritance, so they chose to steal from them. They then spent their life's savings on careless living. Where is the security?

"I'll invest it in the market, real estate, or a business venture. We tell ourselves that we'll be financially secure. We'll be set for life. But markets have downturns, real estate can depreciate, and business ventures can go sour. Rare is the person with the *Midas touch.* Most of us have lost a dollar or two in any one of those investment opportunities.

More than one person has successfully funded their retirement accounts, paid off the mortgage, and purchased their luxury toys. It's not out of the realm of possibility. Like the rich man in the parable told by Jesus, their storehouse was full, their fire was lit, and they believed they were secure. *"Now I will sit back, relax, and enjoy my prosperity*

(Luke 12:19)." But then the parable became their story. *"Fool, this very night your soul will be required of you* (Luke 12:20)."

Jesus said, *"Seek first the kingdom of God and his righteousness* (Matthew 6:33)." Even on our American currency we print, *In God We Trust*. Money can do a lot of things for us. It is a medium of exchange. It has no value beyond what we can exchange it for. It can be exchanged for goods and services. It cannot purchase security. To the contrary, the greater our wealth, the more insecure we become.

I remember leading a Bible study for a women's group on tithing. The question was asked as to whether or not we trusted God to provide for our necessities in life. I shall never forget one woman's response to that question. She was obviously no stranger to the luxuries in life. Her reply was classic, "Oh, I trust God, but I don't trust Him to keep me in the style to which I've grown accustomed."

At what point do we cease to own our possessions and our possessions begin to own us?

Have you ever lost everything you had? People that have had their homes destroyed by wind, water, or fire have known such an experience. Think, all the things that you

50

chose, paid for with hard-earned dollars, insured, polished, and cleaned – gone.

The pain of loss is real. The grief can be unbelievable. One only has to look at the faces of people suffering such a loss on the nightly news. It's amazing how much we can invest of ourselves in stuff. It's just amazing how much it hurts when it's taken from us.

Several years ago I had just such an experience. It was not the result of a natural disaster. The experience, however, was just as real. It's a strange feeling to return to your home to discover that your silver, china, crystal, paintings on the wall, oriental rugs, music system, television, even your automobile are gone.

I now recognize that the experience of losing my possessions was one of the most valuable lessons in my life. It was through that nightmare I came to understand that stuff is only stuff. Money is only money. There are things much more important. Losing one's stuff is a crash course in priority setting and learning to let go.

The peace that passes understanding, serenity, contentment, joy... these are discovered only when one understands they have absolutely nothing to do with labels, money, or possessions.

The writer of *Ecclesiastes* reminds us, "*He who loves money shall never have enough. The foolishness of thinking that wealth brings happiness! The more you have the more you spend right up to the limits of your income* (Ecclesiastes 5:10)."

> **Money will buy:**
> **A bed, but not sleep;**
> **Books, but not brains;**
> **Food, but not an appetite;**
> **A house, but not a home;**
> **Medicine, but not health;**
> **Luxuries, but not culture;**
> **Amusement, but not happiness;**
> **A crucifix, but not a Savior.**

We are free to enjoy our possessions only when we understand that we don't really need them. Money and stuff may purchase for us a lifestyle, but they cannot give us life.

Since losing it all, I have once again accumulated a lot of stuff. It's amazing, however, to know from experience that I don't have to have it. It's nice. It amuses me. I enjoy most of my stuff, but I know that in a moment, in a twinkling of an eye, one day it will be taken from me again.

Could this be what Saint Paul was trying to teach us? His words resonate with a spiritual teaching about money and material possessions. *"I know what it is to be in need, and I know what it is to have plenty.... whether well fed or hungry, whether living in plenty or want. I have learned the secret of being content in any and every situation* (Philippians 4:12-13).*"*

Questions To Stimulate Conversation

"Now I will sit back, relax and enjoy my prosperity. Fool, this very night your soul is required of you (Luke 12:20)." If this is true, why do we think that money can buy security? What kind of security?

"The love of money is the first step toward all kinds of sin. Some people have even turned away from God because of this love of it (I Timothy 6:10)." Did the founding fathers have this scripture in mind when they put on our currency, *In God We Trust?* Why or why not? Just why do you think that phrase is on our currency?

Have you ever lost everything? What was it like? How did you survive? If you haven't ever lost everything, have you known anyone who did? What did you learn from them?

If you were only given five minutes to evacuate your home, what items would you take?

CHAPTER SIX

DO YOU PAY EVERYONE BUT YOURSELF?

"Without consultation, plans are frustrated, but with many counselors they succeed (Proverbs 15:22)."

"Where does all the money go?" I've lost count of the frequency that question has been raised by a couple in my pastoral care. Even more astonishing was discovering that that neither spouse knew the answer. Too often, sophisticated, highly intelligent, well-educated, professional people were without the slightest clue as to why the checkbook was overdrawn, the savings (if any at all) depleted, and the credit cards maxed out. The next payday was still a week or more away.

The scripture calls us to accountability. *"For which of you, desiring to build a tower, does not first sit down and count the cost, to see whether he has enough to complete it* (Saint Luke 14:28)?" How does one answer the question - *Where does all the money go? We* need only look at our cancelled checks, receipts, and credit card statements. Every person needs to hold themselves accountable for their monthly expenditures. They can be easily categorized into one of the following commonly held household categories.

Contributions	Savings
Housing and Utilities	Food
Transportation	Clothing
Insurance	Health Care
Long Term Debt	Revolving Credit
Entertainment	Gambling
Education/Professional	Alcohol/Drugs
Miscellaneous	

Where did all the money go?

Simply analyzing and categorizing the expenditures for the past three months will produce a quick answer to the question. It may appear offensive that I've included *gambling, alcohol, and drugs* as categories. Pastoral experience has taught me that it is needed in today's world. In my pastoral ministry, I've discovered far too many that make the casino their first stop on payday. Likewise, the number of folks who stop first at the local marijuana dispensary or liquor store demands these categories be included. Once the analysis is completed, there is only one question that needs to be answered. *Do you like the way you are spending your income? Is it doing what you want it to do?*

I have used this exercise with countless

individuals, in premarital classes, marriage counseling, and stewardship training classes. There are always some notable surprises. One couple was astounded to discover the enormous amount of money they were spending on magazine subscriptions each year. Many were never read. Another was shocked to see how much they were spending at fast food restaurants. One of my favorite revelations came with yet another couple. Each spouse possessed one of those prepaid cards to a coffee vendor. They routinely had it refilled by adding the expense to their bank credit card. It wasn't until we examined their credit card statement that they realized that between the two of them, they were literally spending several hundred dollars each month on *lattes*!

The following chart is a commonly accepted budget guideline. Overall, the guideline is based on the Christian principle of tithing ten percent and saving ten percent. The first check we write each month is in gratitude to God for giving us life and the gifts to exercise our chosen life work. The second check we write is to ourselves. Wouldn't it be gratifying to know that each month you get to pay yourself? The goal is that we only live on eighty percent of our income, net after taxes. If we live on eighty percent of our income, give ten percent, and save ten percent, it's pretty difficult to live beyond our means.

Budget Guidelines After Taxes	
Contributions	5-10%
Savings	5-10%
Housing & Utilities	35%
Food for a Family of Four	10%
Transportation	15%
Clothing & Personal Care	5%
Insurances	5%
Health Care	5%
Entertainment and Recreation	5%
Revolving Credit	5%
Miscellaneous	5%

Obviously, a chart like the one above may require some adjustment according to the various costs of living dictated by regions of the country, the number of children in a family, and circumstances that may be beyond a person's control. The critical exercise is to first determine just what percentage of the household income is being allotted to the respective categories. The second part of the exercise is to bring any expenditure that is outside the agreed upon percentages in line.

A budget and a good financial plan can help us differentiate between our standard of living and the cost of living. They will require us to set priorities and to live within our incomes.

The book of *Proverbs* states, *"The wise person saves for the future, but the foolish spend whatever they get* (Proverbs 21:20)*."* We Americans have not been taught the value of saving money. The wise person's finances will include a savings plan. Savings insure that there will be a cushion for unexpected emergencies like the loss of a job, major repair on our house or car, new appliances, or a sudden illness. Second, savings allow us to borrow from ourselves, interest-free, when a loan is required for significant purchases. And third, savings provide opportunity for investing in the future rather than borrowing against it.

A disturbing study was released in 2015 by Fidelity investments. Their research revealed that close to one-half of us, forty-eight percent have *no idea* how much money we need to save and invest in order to maintain our current lifestyle in retirement.

The general counsel is that every person should have four funds for savings and investment. The immediate need is to establish an *emergency fund.* This should be an untouchable fund. Its purpose is to cover living expenses for three to six months should you become unemployed. The second fund is for your *retirement*. The third is for you and/or your children's *education*. The fourth is *an Acquisition Fund*. This fund has a directed purpose. These savings are for a down payment on a house, the purchase of an automobile, a vacation, or some other acquisition.

The issue for those fortunate enough to be employed in their chosen endeavor is not the cost of living. Most often it is the standard of living. The problem comes when people who make $50,000 dollars a year want to live as if their income is $60,000 dollars. This problem does not seem to diminish with an increase in resources. I've counseled couples who should be able to live extremely well on $150,000 dollars a year, but their standard of living would have been more compatible with an income twice that amount.

I have a confession. I occasionally buy a lottery ticket. As I anticipate my lucky numbers hitting the mark, my mind dreams of the wonderful things I could do with the jackpot.

A recent study by *The National Endowment for Financial Education* has cast a shadow on my dreams of winning millions. Their research discovered that seventy percent of the people that suddenly receive a large sum of money lose it within just a few short years. There are some horrible stories around lottery winners that include betrayal, theft, drugs, divorce, and murder.

The interesting part of the study is that the people that were good money managers before winning the lottery managed their winnings well. Those that lost their fortunes were victims of their own inability to manage their finances before winning the lottery.

Where does all the money go? It's an easily answered question. What do we want our money to purchase for us? The determining factor is to separate the cost of living from our chosen standard of living. In examining our own stewardship, what keeps us from meeting our saving and charitable giving goals?

The ultimate life question is not answered by what we have accumulated, but by what we have given.

Questions To Stimulate Conversation

Do you disagree with any of the suggested budget guidelines?

If both spouses in your marriage are employed outside the home, have you agreed on just how each will share in the household budget responsibilities? Have you agreed on what amount will remain for you each to spend individually as you choose? If not, perhaps you should do it now.

If either or both of you are divorced or widowed, have you drawn up trusts or have a written agreement on what amount will be shared as a marital asset and the percentage or amount reserved for yourself and your children? Have you shared this information with all your children? If not, perhaps you should do it now.

Have you discussed just how you will share or not share any inheritance either of you might receive? If not, perhaps you should do it now.

CHAPTER SEVEN

WHEN IS FLYING COACH A LUXURY?

"A wise man thinks ahead; a fool doesn't, and even brags about it
(Proverbs 13:16)."

I had to get up at 3:30 in the morning to drive to the Ontario/LAX Airport one hour from my home. I had purchased my ticket online. It was the best deal I could find. To do so meant I had to rise early, find a parking spot in long-term parking, and ride the bus to the terminal. While my plane for the east coast was scheduled to depart at 6:00 a.m., I thought I had given myself plenty of time. Even the best-laid plans can go awry. Oh well, the line at security was longer than I had projected. Then I was singled out for an advanced security check. I made it to my gate just as my flight was being called. I scurried on board, passing through first class. I couldn't help but notice these particular passengers had already been served a beverage of their choice.

My seat was just beyond first class in coach. My heart sank when I discovered that my assigned seat was between two other men who each matched or exceeded my own two hundred pounds. It confirmed my belief that every airline is possessed by a computer devil. Their only task is to insure that three men weighing at least two hundred pounds or more will end up packed together on every flight. Of course, the ever-decreasing seat space would be crowded even if three ninety-five pound supermodels that had eaten nothing but lettuce leaves for the past week were assigned the same seats. With a sigh, I wiggled into the space. The armrests on either side of me were already occupied. I closed my eyes, trying to ignore the hunger pangs welling up in my stomach. For the next four and one-half hours this would be my lot in life.

The plane lifted off safely and I uttered a quick prayer of thanksgiving. By the time we had reached our cruising altitude I was starved. The flight attendant announced that cabin service would begin in a few minutes. "This morning we are offering you a choice of beverages and a breakfast bar. Cocktails are available and correct change would be appreciated." The smell of fresh coffee swept through the airplane. From the other side of the curtain, I heard the flight attendant in first class asked a passenger a question that seared itself into my hunger-tortured body. "Would you like Eggs Benedict, fresh salmon and scrambled eggs, or eggs and pancakes?"

It seemed like we were about to fly over the Mississippi River before the flight attendant came to my fellow seatmates and me. With a nod of gratitude I took a cup of hot coffee from him. I retrieved a honey and oat energy bar from the basket he extended to me. The breakfast bar was as hard as a rock. It didn't matter. I was too hungry not to eat it. As I did, the aroma of the hot breakfasts being eaten by the ten passengers just two feet from me in first class swept over the one hundred fifty of us flying coach.

I decided to do some math. There were ten people in first class. Let's say they each paid fifteen hundred dollars for their tickets. I figured my fellow passengers and I had each paid between three hundred fifty and four hundred dollars for ours. That meant that the breakfast and wider seat that I so wanted at that very moment were being sold for well over a thousand dollars more than my cramped quarters and dry breakfast bar.

The exercise was moot. The only way I could have afforded the price of the first class ticket at the time was to charge it and pay it out in installments. But those installment payments for that first class seat would also mean that I'd have to cut back other places in order to live within my means. Tickets to see my beloved Dodgers would have to wait. Restaurant meals would no longer be an option. And that new suit, well, it too would just have to wait. All of that would have to be tossed aside before I could even consider the sacrifices my family would have to make in order for me to fly first class on this one trip.

It was then that it hit me. Flying coach was a luxury. By flying coach, I was able to protect and preserve the other luxuries that I so appreciated in my life and that of my family. When there are limited resources, it's best not to stretch the limits. Life is about choices. I had made mine.

Often it is not the cost of living
that causes us problems.
It is the standard of living
we choose.

A Christian understanding of money sets limits and helps us to learn to prioritize expending it. The good choices are the ones that bring a sense of gratitude. Our choices need not end up as burdens. Those who have a difficult time being thankful in the midst of abundance have not yet learned this lesson.

As I sat squeezed between my two seatmates on that airplane flight with the smell of the hot breakfast being served in first class tormenting me, I was faced with the choices I'd made in life. If I had chosen another profession, perhaps a first class ticket wouldn't even make a dent in my bank account. Or if I'd chosen to pursue a career with a prosperous corporation, I could have charged my wider seat and hot breakfast to a corporate expense account. But I chose to be a priest. I chose to follow my heart. In the choosing, I was able to do that which I felt I was meant to do on this fragile planet. In the choosing, it also meant that my financial resources would be more limited than those other career paths would have afforded me. It meant that for my entire life I would have to set priorities and make choices with the resources I had earned. Fifteen hundred dollar breakfasts would not be a viable option for me.

A good way to get a handle on the choices we've made with our money is to visit our attics and storage booths. Take a close look at all the "stuff" we just had to have. At the time, it was irresistible. Perhaps it would make us happy. Maybe the neighbors would be impressed. We thought it was going to bring us great fun at the time. Now, it just sits in boxes collecting dust. It takes up space and does none of the things for us we thought it would do.

In order to make wise choices with the money we do have and establish priorities, I would suggest that we divide our choices into the following three categories.

NECESSITIES are the goods and services we absolutely must have to survive.

These are the basic building blocks of life. They are without label or prestige. They impress no one. They sustain us and nourish us.

CONVENIENCES are not required for living, but they make life more comfortable. These too are without label or prestige. They impress no one and will be envied by few. They simply make our daily tasks a little nicer.

LUXURIES always come with a label. We often purchase them for the prestige value. They are not necessary. They have absolutely no utilitarian purpose that could not be served by a less expensive product without the label. Luxuries are most often purchased not for what they can provide, but for whom they can impress. Luxuries are status symbols. Luxuries are touted as *top-of-the-line, one-of-a-kind, an original, the best money can buy, first class,* or one of the ugliest words in any language, *exclusive.*

When ambition ends,
happiness begins.
Thomas Merton

What would happen if we began to look at the material goods of this world from the standpoint of function? What is the particular item's function? Will it help me be more effective in my profession? Will it contribute to my physical health, my mental or spiritual well-being? Do I want it simply to impress some unseen audience in my world? Or is the purchase an attempt to prove that I am a person of worth -- successful?

Maybe an even better question is this one. *How much will I be able sell it for in a garage sale?* I think that's a good question we might ask ourselves before giving in to the pressure of advertising to purchase something we really don't need. Impulse buys might be evaluated with the same question. Once we tire of it, *how much will I be able sell it for in a garage sale?* Perhaps the answer to that question determines the real value of the item.

Questions To Stimulate Conversation

When you made your career choice, did you consider the income ceiling that came with it? Why or why not?

Do you feel embarrassed or humiliated when you have to help your children accept that you may not have the financial resources that some of their friends' parents possess?

When you examined your expenditures for the last three months, what percentage of your money went to items that would be categorized as luxuries? Did they do for you what you wanted them to do, or have you already tired of them?

Before making any purchase, should we ask ourselves - *How much will I be able sell it for in a garage sale?*

CHAPTER EIGHT

WAS EBENEZER SCROOGE GREEDY?

"Keep your life free from the love of money, and be content with what you have (Hebrews 13:5)."

I have known frugal people. They try to stretch every dollar to its limit. The phrases surrounding these thrifty souls are numerous: *As tight as the bark on a tree. Squeeze a penny until it screams. So tight they squeak when they walk. Waste not, want not* is their mantra. On television, Jack Benny portrayed a penny-pinching miser. It was said that *he laughed all the way to the bank*.

It would come as a shock to most who pride themselves on being frugal that the line between their self-appointed virtue and the sin of greed is a thin one indeed. In the Church, we often present frugality as the antithesis of materialism. The truth of the matter is that frugality and greed are two sides of the same coin. Charles Dickens portrayed Ebenezer Scrooge as the ultimate penny-pincher. His sin, however, was greed. His salvation did not come until he began to let go of that to which he squeezed so tightly.

During my tenure as a parish rector, I presided at countless vestry and board meetings. From time to time, I have seen persons who quickly appointed themselves as *Keepers of the Treasury*. As the watchdogs of the parish finances, they often successfully argued for doing things as *economically* as possible. I have also watched subsequent vestries have to go back and spend even more money undoing the frugal decision and having to do it again.

Stewardship is seldom the issue for the overly frugal. **Stewardship is managing that which God has given us in a way that can produce the most fruit.** The parable of the talents is such a teaching. *So I was afraid and went out and hid your gold in the ground. See, here is what belongs to you.' His master replied, 'You wicked, lazy servant! So you knew that I harvest where I have not sown and gather where I have not scattered seed? Well then, you should have put my money on deposit with the bankers, so that when I returned I would have received it back with interest* (Matthew 25:25)." The sin of the frugal steward was holding onto the money. He buried his coin in the ground.

Instead of paying someone else to do it, the frugal would prefer to hold onto their money and do it themselves. That reminds me of a plumbing advertisement - *Pay us to fix it right today or we can build you a new one for twice as much tomorrow.* Perhaps the best motto I saw for a plumber was this one. *If you watch me fix it, I'll double the price. If you insist on helping me fix it, the price will be tripled.* The overly frugal often end up costing themselves and others more in the long run. When they cut corners they sometimes fail to realize that the ends still have to meet.

Rare is the person facing major surgery that will request *the cheapest surgeon they can find*. Most of us would want the best money can buy. In most every facet of our lives, we will want the best return for our dollar.

I once heard a bishop admonish a congregation for the shameful salaries they were paying their clergy and staff. He actually accused them of giving in to the very greed they preached against. He insisted they wanted something for nothing. He suggested they were burying their financial resources instead of using them to produce fruit for the Kingdom of God. To lighten the moment, he concluded, "Remember, if you pay peanuts you're going to get monkeys".

A classic Jack Benny skit is a robbery scene. The thief says to Jack, "Your money or your life!" Jack stands in silence. The thief yells, "Well?"

Jack taps his cheek and responds, "I'm thinking. I'm thinking."

Frugality simply must be brought into the light of day. At the heart of frugality may very well be the sin of greed. Regardless of the name frugality calls itself, or the mask it chooses to wear, greed has no place in the life of a Christian. The most dangerous evils are the ones that disguise themselves as virtues. Frugality and greed have much in common.

Questions To Stimulate Conversation

Have you ever served on a vestry or a board with a *Keeper of the Treasury* that always wanted to do things as cheaply as possible? What were the results?

At what point do you think frugality becomes greed?

Ebenezer Scrooge is often thought of as the ultimate penny-pincher. Do you think it is more accurate to think of him as greedy?

CHAPTER NINE

CAN YOUR BORROW YOURSELF OUT OF DEBT?

"The rich rule over the poor, and the borrower becomes the lender's slave (Proverbs 22:7)."

It's just so easy. The young clerk asks, "Would you like to save twenty percent on your purchase today? If you will apply for one of our credit cards, we can save you twenty percent on all of your purchases today. It will only take a couple of minutes to complete the application."

There are other easy-application credit cards that promise us airline miles or cash back. If we apply for their credit card, we can get a free airline ticket to any city in the continental United States. Or to sweeten the deal, how would you like an all expense paid three days in Honolulu, Hawaii? Zero percent interest is offered. That is, until it escalates to 28% after ninety days. No payments for the first six months. Now, who wouldn't want that?

The interest clock on debt never ends. It runs twenty-four hours a day, seven days a week. Yet, too many people have deceived themselves into believing that it's possible to borrow themselves out of debt.

I have read that the typical American is three weeks from bankruptcy because of debt, not out of necessity, but debt as a way of life. Such debt is the result of the inability to postpone purchases, the need for instant gratification, or attempting a lifesyle beyond one's actual income level.

Credit card debt has Americans making minimum payments on things purchased long ago and forgotten. After interest charges are tacked on, one is often shocked to discover that they owe more on a product than its actual market value. The business world calls this being "upside down".

Using the Visa Card to make a payment on the Master Card is simply digging a deeper hole. Credit card companies are currently deceiving some borrowers into believing that they can get zero percent interest loans. Borrowers pay an initial three to five percent transaction fee up front. **That is interest.** If the borrower fails to pay the entire amount by the expiration date, all the accumulated interest of fourteen percent or more will be due.

Leading up to the last financial crisis, homeowners were encouraged to borrow against the equity in their homes. Far too many did that very thing. They increased the debt on their houses in order to purchase boats, automobiles, swimming pools, and recreational vehicles. When the bottom fell out, many of those same people lost their homes.

Today, seniors are being encouraged to get a reverse mortgage on their homes. Basically, it is another form of a home equity loan. No payments are due as long as you live in your home, but a loan is still a loan. They carry with them expensive closing costs and other fees. Those executing the loan receive a commission and must be paid.

Beyond that, many reverse mortgages carry other dangers. While the soothing voices of the paid actors on the television ads make reverse mortgages sound appealing, seniors need to see them for what they are. They are an equity loan on your home for sure, but they are one that may be fraught with danger.

Some reverse mortgages may require that they be repaid immediately. Failure to do so can lead to a foreclosure. Some loans specify exactly the number of days, weeks, and/or months the property can sit vacant. Here's an example. If you have to go to the hospital or assisted living for the specified time period, the lender just may be able to require immediate repayment on the house because it's unoccupied. If the loan is not paid, the house can be sold right out from under you.

There is the further possibility that you or your spouse could end up homeless. In cases where only one spouse's name is on the reverse mortgage contract, the house may be sold if the borrower dies. All reverse mortgages require immediate repayment on the death of the borrower. If that cannot be done from other assets, the house will be sold, leaving the surviving spouse homeless.

Before signing any loan document, it's wise to have an attorney go over it with you. Before taking on any debt of any kind, it is equally wise to consult a financial planner for advice. Professional financial planners can be invaluable counselors when it comes to getting our financial house in order, making a savings plan, and helping us secure a safe and secure retirement.

The Bible is crystal clear on debt. *"Owe no one anything, except to love one another* (Romans 13:8)." Likewise, the Bible is clear on the necessity of paying back debt: *"Evil people borrow and cannot pay it back! But the good man returns what he owes with some extra besides* (Psalm 37:21)." *"Don't withhold repayment of your debts. Don't say 'some other time,' if you can pay now* (Proverbs 3:27, 28)." Proverbs 17:18 also makes it clear. *"It is poor judgment to countersign another's note, to become responsible for their debt."*

Even after keeping all this Biblical counsel in mind, one fact remains. For most of us, debt is a part of life. Not many of us can pay cash for a home. Thus, a mortgage is necessary. My studies indicate that a good rule of thumb for debt within one's means can be justified for a home, business, and education. The prudent guide would suggest that debt is justified on appreciating assets only. But then again, who can afford to pay cash for a dependable automobile? When only minimum wage jobs are available upon graduation in the current market, how does one justify going into debt for a university education costing thousands of dollars? Too many graduates discover that their degree is worthless in the current marketplace.

A theology of money needs to include a plan that will keep debt in its proper place. Any credit card that cannot be paid off monthly is a costly liability. A plan needs to be developed to quickly retire all but long-term debt on a home to live in. When possible, fifteen-year mortgages are highly desirable over thirty-year ones. Making even the smallest additional payments each month on one's mortgage can radically expedite the retirement of the mortgage debt by several years. And finally, a firm resolution needs to be made to live within one's income.

Applying for multiple credit cards is far too easy. It can also be the foundation stone for financial disaster. Our own government expends more than it receives. Our elected leaders continue to borrow from generations yet to come. They are apparently unable to say "no". We Christians must refrain from emulating our elected government leaders. King Solomon, some 3000 years ago, wrote what just may be the bottom line on debt, *"Just as the rich rule the poor, so the borrower is servant to the lender* (Proverbs 22:7)."

Questions To Stimulate Conversation

Respond to the following Scripture.

"Evil men borrow and cannot pay it back! But the good man returns what he owes with some extra besides (Psalm 37:21)*."*

Now discuss this passage.

"It is poor judgment to countersign another's note, to become responsible for his debt (Proverbs 17:18)*."*

Does the following passage support the teachings in this chapter?

"The wise man saves for the future, but the foolish man spends whatever he gets (Proverbs 21:20)*."*

Do you consult a professional financial planner? Is it wise to employ one?

CHAPTER TEN

ARE YOUR CHILDREN BECOMING FINANCIAL SNOWFLAKES?

"The younger son got together all he had, set off for a distant country and there squandered his wealth in wild living (Luke 15:13)."

The descriptive word *Snowflake* rose to popular use during the 2016 political season. It described the reaction of high school and college students who simply could not deal with the outcome of that election. The word *Snowflake* can serve an illustrative purpose in this chapter. I've chosen to use the word and all that it describes without any reference to the election itself, but to what I perceived as a very disturbing pattern of behavior.

In the real world of employment there are no safe places. Your salary will not be granted as a participation trophy. You will be expected to show up to work and produce. If a customer or client is rude to you, your employer is not going to provide you with crayons or a therapy dog. And if you get a new supervisor that you don't like, you won't be given time off to organize a protest march. Your year-end bonus will not be awarded because you are a nice person. You will be expected to excel in your tasks.

Regardless of the profession chosen, there will be fellow employees that undercut you to management. Multiple competitors will challenge you and try to take your clients from you. If you perform your job in a mediocre fashion, your employer will dispatch you into the dark night of unemployment. Trying to protect our children from these realities will do them a great disservice.

In the real world, if we have failed to prepare our children for it, the axiom of *dog eat dog* can be a shock. Financially, parents should strive to teach their children how to survive in the real world. They will need more than a formal education and training for their chosen profession. They will also need the tools and experience of actually being able to work in a highly competitive world. The ultimate goal is to teach them how to be self-sufficient financially. This is especially needed if we are no longer able or available to bail them out.

My first job was selling *Grit Magazines*. It was a Saturday magazine that would arrive at my house on Friday afternoon. Any copies that I failed to sell were my responsibility. My profits were dependent on selling every magazine. My entire Saturday was consumed with making sales calls in my neighborhood. That was my first entrepreneurial venture. I was twelve years old.

I grew up in a family that was strongly committed to the work ethic. It was instilled in me at an early age. I was never given an allowance. If I wanted something extra, I could earn money by doing chores around the house in addition to those already assigned. I could mow the lawn or rake leaves in the neighborhood. Often there were matching funds. Once I wanted a camera. I was told, "You save half and we'll give you the other half."

Throughout my high school, college, and seminary years my parents helped, but they expected me to do my share by working at part-time jobs in addition to my studies. It has been an exercise in holy pride for me to think about the part-time jobs that helped make my education possible. They included working in the hay fields for five cents a bale, delivering newspapers, selling doughnuts door to door, being a Western Union boy, working in a butcher shop, serving as a hotel clerk, sacking powdered milk for the military, selling vacuum cleaners, working door to door selling Fuller Brush products, selling jewelry, driving an ambulance, working in a mortuary, and wait for it, working as a beer bartender.

Those multiple jobs may be the product of a value system unique to the Midwest. I am grateful for it. I am still amazed by the expectations of some of the young candidates for employment I interviewed as a parish rector. Several prospects demanded starting salaries comparable to those being paid senior staff. Too often they expected paid leave time that would have basically made them part-time employees. A couple of candidates viewed the Church as their backup plan. If they managed their own personal finances poorly, they believed we should take up an offering to bail them out of their self-created mess. One even blatantly insisted, *"We actually owed them"*. Scripture teaches otherwise - *"If any won't work, then they should not eat* (2 Thessalonians 3:10).*"*

Teaching financial independence is the obligation of every parent. Most all the kids in the neighborhood I grew up in delivered newspapers, mowed lawns, or earned money through other part-time employment. What a contrast to the teenager today that expects their parents to buy them a new sports car. We all want our children to have it better than we had it. That's only natural. If we indulge all the wants our children bring to us, we may deprive them of something that is much more important and lasting.

Overindulged children do not know the satisfaction of working on a goal, saving, and anticipating their achievement. They are deprived of the experience of knowing the satisfaction of having done it themselves. They are deprived of the knowledge that they don't have to have their every want satisfied in order to be happy. And of even greater importance, they will not develop the confidence to provide for themselves.

All of my four children have given me countless moments of pride. One that stands out in this area is when my oldest son wanted me to drive him to a local restaurant to apply for a job as a busboy. When we pulled up in front of the establishment he stated emphatically, "Now Dad, I want you to stay here in your car. I'm going to do this for myself." I remained in my car uttering silent prayers for his success for what seemed like hours. I know it was only minutes. I could tell from the look on his face when he came out of the restaurant that he had gotten the job. That's a feeling that spoiled children will never know.

Scripture counsels us to provide for our children. *"When a good person dies, he leaves an inheritance* (Proverbs 13:22)." But experience has shown that inherited wealth has destroyed as many people as it has helped. Marriages have absolutely ended in divorce and families broken apart over inheritance disputes.

Andrew Carnegie wrote, "No man has the right to handicap his son with such a burden as great wealth. He must face this question squarely: *Will my fortune be safe* with my boy and will my boy be safe with my fortune?"

Proverbs 20:21 issues this caution, *"An inheritance gained hurriedly in the beginning will not be blessed in the end."*

If we have an inheritance to leave our children, it's our responsibility to help them develop a Christian theology of money. In the long run, the practical theology of money we give them will be of more value than the inheritance. It may very well be the best way to safeguard the inheritance itself.

Scripture clearly teaches a work ethic. *"Whatever you do, do your work heartily as for the Lord rather than for self* (Colossians 3:23)*."*

The Scriptures make it clear that work is a part of life. *"Let everyone be sure that they are doing their very best, for then they will have the personal satisfaction of work well done* (Galatians 6:4)."

Parents do have the responsibility of providing for their children. At the same time, teaching responsible independence is the obligation of every parent. Teaching children the satisfaction of work well done begins early in life. Teaching them how to provide for themselves is a critical parental goal.

Overindulged children are deprived of the experience of doing for themselves. Teaching children to establish goals, set financial priorities, make choices from many possibilities, and realizing their dreams for themselves is a parental responsibility. The ultimate lesson is learning that they do not have to have their every want satisfied in order to be happy.

I should think that most every parent with limited resources can recall unhappy moments in the toy store. What was supposed to be a fun trip to buy a surprise turns into a nightmare. Usually this occurs when our little darling has picked out a surprise with a price tag on it that far surpasses our planned expenditure. The words *no* and *choose something else* are not often met with *Sure, daddy. Let me look*. My experience in those situations has most often been marked with whining, tears, and an occasional tantrum thrown in for the benefit of the other store customers.

The words *we can't afford it* or *that's more than we want to spend* or even *that's outside our budget* are not unkind words. Most every one of us thinks we would like to give the objects of our devotion everything they think they want. The popular definition of true love, after all, (parental or otherwise) is marked by the amount of stuff we can overwhelm our loved ones with. They should want for nothing.

I still remember living out this scene with one of our children in a music store.

She had selected three CDs. The total cost of the three CDs exceeded sixty dollars. I responded, "You must choose one of them. I only brought enough cash for one."

My sweet child, having studied in the federal government's school of economics, replied, "Why not write a check or charge them?"

Where does a seven year old learn these things? Again, in the face of tears and a not so subtle pout, I held my ground – "Choose".

Perhaps, to an observer, I wasn't being a loving father. Obviously, I could have written a check or used my charge card. Clearly, the sixty dollars was not even the real issue. The issue for me was helping my child learn how to set boundaries, to set priorities, to make choices.

I believe that those who are given everything end up appreciating nothing. Eventually my child made a choice and even managed an appreciative, *Thank you, daddy*. As further evidence that no good deed goes unpunished, I had to listen to that one CD over and over and over again every time we were in the car together. I thought they never were going to *Free Willy.*

We parents will have a difficult time teaching our children to set limits, prioritize among choices, and live within their means if we can't do it for ourselves. The test of our ability to say *no* to ourselves may very well be reflected in our ability to say *no* to our children. This won't be easy. The typical high school graduate today has spent 10,800 hours in the classroom and 15,000 hours in front of the television. They have watched between fifty and one hundred commercials a day. That doesn't include the ones that pop up on the Internet.

Economics is first learned in the home. The pressure to keep up with the neighbor's children can be devastating. The tearful cry *everyone's doing it, going, or buying it* can go right to our parental guilt. One of the most unloving things we can do for our children is to give in to that competitive pressure. *We can't afford it - that's more than we want to spend*, and *it's outside our budget* – these are not words of parental abuse or neglect; these can be words of love. Coming to terms with financial limits and making choices within those limits is one of the most valuable lessons we can teach those we love.

Even if we have abundant financial resources, parents wisely establish monetary limits. Loving parents teach their children how to establish priorities and make choices with the money they do have and not with the money they wish they had.

I fully realize that such a concept may be socially unacceptable and embarrassing in some circles. But a responsible expenditure of money should not be determined by social pressure. The phrase *we can't afford it* is a great deal more desirable than the confession *we bought it, but now we can't pay for it*.

My parents loved me so much that they did not give me everything that I wanted.
They taught me how to provide for myself.

Christian parents will want to teach their children responsible independence. The best teacher is experience. Here are some suggested ways to do just that:

1. Give them chores to do around the house and hold them accountable for doing them. These chores are the responsibility they have as a member of the family. Their allowance, if any, should not be attached to accomplishing these chores. Learning the satisfaction and pride in a job well done can start at an early age.

2. Learn to say *no*. Do not give in to their every whim, want, demand, or temper tantrum.

3. Offer to match what they save for something they want. And on occasion, they should pay for their want completely with the money they have earned.

4. Encourage them to work for other people. The most productive classroom you can offer just may be part-time jobs that do not interfere with their studies.

5. They should take responsibility for turning off lights, water, recycling, and not making unnecessary car trips in order to conserve energy, and assist with the family finances. These can also help them learn to be good stewards of our fragile planet.

6. Teach them to share what they earn with others by occasionally using some of their own money to buy presents for friends, siblings, and parents.

7. Start at an early age teaching them to put some of the money they have earned in the church offering plate.

8. Teach them how to save a portion of the money they earn for a future want or event.

Scripture offers the following counsel. *"Train up a child in the way that they should go and when they are older they will not depart from it* (Proverbs 22:6)." Self-serving adults who believe the world owes them a living were not born with that attitude. They got their training from someone. Christian parents want to try to insure that their home is not such a classroom.

Questions To Stimulate Conversation

At what age should children begin chores in the home? What type of chores would be appropriate?

What are the factors that turn children into self-indulging adults?

What would you add to the list of suggestions for teaching children and teens responsibility?

When do you think it is acceptable to be a bit extravagant when granting your children's wishes?

CHAPTER ELEVEN

WHAT TYPE OF GIVER ARE YOU?

"A poor widow came and put in two copper coins. 'Truly I say to you, this poor widow put in more than all the rich contributors; for they put in out of their surplus, but she put in all she owned (Mark 12: 43-44).*"*

It may come as a surprise to discover that poor people are more charitable than the wealthy. In 2009, *The McClatchy Newspapers* conducted a study on charitable giving. They discovered that the poor donate the highest percentage of their income to charity. The poor surveyed contributed an average of 4.3 percent of their income to charity. The rich people surveyed only averaged 2.1 percent.

There was some even more shocking information released by *Forbes Magazine*. In their 2012 study, they discovered that in light of the great recession, the wealthy were giving less to charity while the poor increased their giving. A study done by *The Chronicle of Philanthropy* found this to be true. They discovered that the average American who earned $200,000 dollars or more gave nearly 5% less to charity in 2012 than they did in 2006. The study further discovered that Americans that made less than $100,000 dollars gave 5% more over this same time period.

The most revealing discovery was that the poorest in our country that took home less than $25,000 dollars actually increased their giving by nearly 17 percent during these same years. The study further disclosed that those who increased their giving the most in all of the categories were people of faith. The article categorized the most generous as *religious people.* During that recession, the very wealthy donated an average of only 1.3 percent of their income.

In an article widely circulated on the Internet, *The Atlantic Magazine* reported that "wealth affects not only how much money is given but to whom it is given." The poor tend to give to religious organizations and social service charities that actually feed the hungry and assist the needy. The wealthy prefer to support private prep schools, colleges and universities, music and art programs, and museums.

Of the fifty largest individual gifts to public charities in 2012, thirty-four went to educational institutions. The vast majority of the gifts went to colleges and universities, like Harvard, Columbia, and Berkeley, that cater to the nation's and the world's elite. Museums and arts organizations such as the Metropolitan Museum of Art received nine of the major gifts, with the remaining donations spread over medical facilities and fashionable charities like the Central Park Conservancy. Not a single one of them went to a social service organization. And none went to any charity that primarily meets the needs of the poor and the dispossessed. More gifts from this group went to elite prep schools than to any other charity. The most prominent social-service groups in our country were neglected. Charities like the United Way, the Salvation Army, and Feeding America did not receive a single contribution from this list of donors.

After contrasting the charitable giving of both the wealthy and the poor, I have learned that in faith communities there are some sharp giving distinctions. Within the Church, I have discovered there are basically four giving types.

The first I call the **Welfare Recipients.** These are people who give absolutely nothing to the Church. Yet, these are the very same people who expect the Church to be there for their convenience and to respond to their every whim. Often, these non-givers are quite active in the political affairs of the congregation. The bottom line, however, is that they are on welfare. They are feeding off the generosity of the other parish members.

The second group I call **Tippers**. The tipper puts some loose change or a few dollars in the offering plate when they attend.

Hopefully, they are more generous to the hospitality workers in restaurants than they are to the Church. One of the embarrassing experiences as a parish priest was to discover that during an audit, the amount reported by Tippers to Internal Revenue seldom matched the cash contributions recorded by the parish treasurer. Even then, it was often less than one percent of their annual income.

The Control Giver is the third type. The Control Giver uses their contribution to purchase control, power, or recognition for themselves. As long as things are going their way and the clergy are paying sufficient attention to them, then they can be quite generous. Storm warnings need to be posted! If the controlled giver becomes unhappy with the clergy, a decision of the board, the diocese or national church, or they no longer feel in control, their giving can dry up in an instant.

Some think they can control the decisions of the Church by withholding their support to the local congregation. Still others, like the Pharisees of old, will give only when there is sufficient fanfare. Then there are those that will give only so long as the priest acts as their personal chaplain.

Sadly, any substantive gift from Control Givers often requires naming a room or an entire building in their honor. At the very least, they're going to demand a brass plaque displayed in a prominent location. I heard a priest friend say about these control givers, "God loves a cheerful giver, but He will take money from a grouch."

The Fair Share Giver is the person who wants the church to function effectively and efficiently. They also want to pay their fair share. These often take the annual operating costs of the parish and divide by the number of giving units. They feel this is their fair share. Sometimes they simply try to give the equivalent of the average annual pledge in the parish. However they figure it, again, my experience has been that it is usually considerably less than the dues to their private club or the amount they spend on a hobby in a given year.

The Tither is the person who strives to return ten percent of their annual income to the work and ministry of the Church. For the tither, giving is a spiritual expression of their internal faith. They believe in the work of Jesus. They own the importance of worship, discipleship, pastoral care, evangelism, and caring for the poor. These things are the true mission of the Church. They understand them to be their mission as a Christian.

Beyond that, the tither gives as an expression of gratitude to God. When they consider their life, they focus not on what they don't have, but what they do have. Their tithe is an expression of their love and

100

gratitude in the same way that a gift is an expression of love and gratitude to one's child or spouse.

I have discovered that tithing cannot be sold. It is the inevitable fruit of a deeper spiritual experience. One grows into tithing as one grows in their relationship with God. I have never known a tither that had to declare bankruptcy. Because they are tithing, they are already living within their means. It's not tithing that makes this happen. No, it is the spiritual health of their soul. They have developed a Christian theology of money. Their resources are budgeted to include the tithe. For many, the tithe is the first check written.

The tithe may be the single greatest indicator of the health of our souls. A tither gives out of their own spiritual need, not because the Church needs the money. The tither gives because they need to give. Their soul's health will not allow them to do otherwise.

Rare is the person or household that can immediately begin giving ten percent of their financial resources to church and charities. Exercising Christian stewardship over our finances requires that we first set goals. These goals are best achieved through the household budget. Establishing goals of saving ten percent and giving ten percent may require that we must first bring other expenditures into line and retire debt. So while we may not all be able to immediately tithe, we can all immediately begin to **strive to tithe.** We do so by beginning with a goal of two to five percent and then increase it as we get the other line items in our household budgets under control.

I will never forget one young husband in my parish during the recession of the mid - 1970s calling his wife with some distressing news. His company had to reduce the salaries of their employees in order to remain viable. After telling her that his salary had been reduced, he tried to brighten the news. He chuckled and told her, "The good news is that we are now tithing!"

The very best monetary news ever given to Christians is the Biblical tithe. The good news is that God does not ask for it all. God only asks us to give ten percent! From the earliest Biblical record, only the tenth portion of the fruits of our labor was to be returned to God.

Our annual tithe is written from our checkbooks. We also have a responsibility to tithe on the funds we keep in our safe deposit boxes. Numerous Christians die every year, leaving trusts and gifts to symphonies, art museums, colleges and schools, but nothing to their Church.

Church futurists state that the local congregation in the future will not be able to survive on the pledge and plate offerings alone. Church leadership today needs to plan for this future reality that may be upon many congregations already. A minimum of twenty percent of the annual ministry budget will need to come from income on endowments. Another ten to twenty percent will need to come from rents, fees, fundraisers, and other entrepreneurial ventures. Every parish leader and congregational member needs to plan today for these changing realities.

The local congregation is the primary household of God. It is in and through the local parish that the faithful worship, hear the Gospel story, are cared for, trained to care, reach out to the least of our brothers and sisters, and invite others to join us in this ministry. This is the ministry of Jesus. It is our ministry.

If the Church of the future is to support ministry at all levels as it has in the past, then endowments for the ministry of the Church are an absolute necessity. Currently in America, we are experiencing one of the greatest intergenerational transfers of wealth in history. Schools, hospitals, universities, and museums have campaigns prepared to assist people with making planned gifts and endowment contributions to their work. The Church must do the same. We aren't asking people to not give to these other good works. No, we are just asking that Christians also remember the work and ministry of the Church in their final distribution of wealth.

A large parish in the Episcopal Diocese of Pennsylvania invited me to speak on planned giving at their stewardship dinner. The senior warden was introducing me to the gathered congregation. He smiled, "It is my honor to introduce Doctor Dennis R. Maynard. He's come all the way from California to tell us how it's easier to tithe to the Church after we're dead!"

It is the Church that celebrated our births, nurtured our faith, and will be with us as we make our transition into the next life. It will be the Church that will be there for our families when we are gone. This ministry is of value. Its benefit is easily demonstrated. Its value is beyond price.

Most every parish church is in need of endowment income. Christians will want to remember the ministry of their parish and diocese in the final distribution of their wealth. In truth, the final distribution of our worldly goods may be the most accurate mirror of what was really important to us in this life.

Questions To Stimulate Conversation

When is it appropriate to adjust one's annual gift to the parish based on the giver's happiness or unhappiness with the pastor or ministry program?

When is it acceptable to recognize a gift to the parish with a brass plaque or naming opportunity?

Should donations to secular charities be included as a part of your annual tithe? Why or why not?

Do you think that beginning a tithing goal with a smaller percentage and increasing it each year is a viable concept? Why or why not?

Do you believe that gifts to exclusive private schools and universities that charge enormous tuitions qualify as a charitable gift? Why or why not?

Do you agree with this statement?
The soul filled with thanksgiving to the Almighty needs to give.

CHAPTER TWELVE

ARE ALL CHARITIES EQUAL?

"Will a person rob God? But you say, 'How have we robbed You?' In your tithes and offerings (Malachi 3:8-9).*"*

When I was a child, my parents would give me a penny to put in the Church offering plate. I have often thought about those pennies. I'm not sure that practice taught me much about giving. First, the money was not mine. My parents gave it to me for that singular purpose. It was a not so subtle form of forced giving. Second, I knew that I could not use the penny for anything else. And third, even as a child, I knew that a penny was not very much money.

The competition for the charitable dollar has also changed. When I started my ministry in the late 1960s, the full Biblical tithe was clearly intended for the local parish. Today, even the most devout no longer accept that premise. There are many very worthwhile endeavors competing for the charitable dollar.

The annual parish letter on stewardship simply does not have the same sway as one of those heart-wrenching charitable appeals that routinely appear on our televisions. The parish newsletter cannot compete with the distraught faces of children, veterans, and animals all in need of our assistance.

There are brochures designed to tear at our heartstrings. Professional and volunteer telephone canvassers are utilized by many charities. Professional fundraisers are often employed by others. Some promise to return a coffee mug, a paperweight, or a bumper sticker in return for your gift. The list of contributors and their level of giving is openly published in programs or magazines. This leads to the subtle pressure that we need to be included in a significant category. The local parish is simply not equipped to compete with the polished marketing tools used by so many worthwhile causes.

One of the most revealing experiences in ministry was discovering a parish where the average annual gift was very modest in contrast to the incomes of the members. I was astounded to learn that some of the most vocal in that parish served on the governing body and had no recordable gift. These same folks preferred using the bequests left to the parish by deceased members for the current ministry program. They were quite literally content to finance the ministry of that parish with the money of dead people

Over the years, I've noticed one more thing that most every parish I've served or consulted with has in common. I call it *The*

Eighty-Twenty Rule. Eighty percent of the funds given to the parish come from twenty percent of the people. That does not devalue the twenty percent contributed by the remaining eighty percent. Many of those giving that twenty percent are truly giving the widow's mite.

Others, however, are content to be members of the *52 Club, i.e., one dollar per week.* Every parish has one. These are the folks that give one dollar a week. These are seldom the widow's mite. Most often the dollar bill is meant as a protest of some parish or denominational program. It might be intended to show their contempt for the denominational authority or senior minister. Others are content to give one dollar a week simply to maintain their membership so they can vote in the annual meeting. Beyond the *52 Club*, it is my observation that in too many congregations, up to forty percent of the membership has no record of giving.

Charity begins at home! We've all heard it. It's a true statement for Christians. Scripture teaches that our families are our primary responsibility. *"If anyone does not provide for his own, and especially for those of his own household, he has denied the faith, and he is considered to be worse than an unbeliever* (I Timothy 5:8)."

Beyond our immediate families, we are responsible for our parish church. Our parish is our *extended family.* The notion that the Church and Christian workers should mirror some sort of poverty is absolutely contrary to the teachings of scripture. *"Pastors who do their work well should be paid well and should be highly appreciated especially those who work hard at both preaching and teaching* (I Timothy 5:17)."

It's difficult to bless the lifestyles of unscrupulous television evangelists, but the image of the poor and starving pastor is compatible only when they are serving a poor and starving people. A financially strapped and struggling church can be acceptable only when the people of the church themselves are financially strapped and struggling. Just as it is our mutual responsibility to see that our family expenditures are responsible and achieve the stated goals, we have this same responsibility when it comes to our parish. The local parish must be transparent when it comes to finances. Every member must have the assurance that their stewardship dollars are achieving the ministry goals of the parish.

The concept of blindly pledging to the parish is contrary to every understanding of stewardship. Stewardship is not just about raising money; it is also being accountable for the way in which the stewardship dollars are spent. We hold accountable that which is important. The opposite of accountability is apathy, or worse, blind faith. The history of the church is checkered with examples of foolish misappropriation of church funds. This mismanagement was made possible simply because the governing boards and the active membership failed to hold those charged with ministry accountable. The ministry goals of the parish need to be clearly defined. Those goals need to be further defined in terms of cost. When the parish asks for an increase in the ministry budget, those needs must be clearly matched with ministry goals and the dollars needed to achieve them.

Generous givers do not always have a surplus of money.
They simply manage their money so that they have a surplus to give.

The third group for which we are responsible is the poor. One third of the population of the world goes to bed hungry every night. Christians cannot turn their backs on the poor. While Jesus reminds us that the poor may always be with us, we must continue to do as we can. Proverbs 28:27 reminds us, *"If you give to the poor, your needs will be supplied. But a curse upon those who close their eyes to poverty."* Here again, responsibility and accountability are a part of stewardship. There are a multitude of ministries and charities that have a goal of helping the poor. It is our responsibility to make sure they are doing that very thing.

I received a telephone solicitation one evening for what I thought was a worthwhile charity to support our local law enforcement. I used a charitable giving website to check on the charity. I was shocked to discover that the widows and orphans of the fallen officers were receiving only a small fraction of the funds donated. Most of it was going to the professional fundraisers.

We have a responsibility to give, but we also have a responsibility to make sure the charity is expending our stewardship dollars wisely. We should not respond to emotional appeals without a clear understanding of just where our contribution is going. That is a critical part of our stewardship responsibility. *We will always hold accountable that which is important to us.*

Before donating to any organization, it is important to check with one of the charity watchdogs to see just where your gift will have the greatest impact. There are three organizations on the Internet that are worth utilizing. There are others that are quite dependable, but I would like to suggest the following: *give.org, charitynavigator.org*, and *charitywatch.org.*

Those three are dependable resources that I currently use and trust. These excellent websites evaluate charities by looking at just what percentage of your charitable gift actually reaches the individuals that the organizations claim to support.

There is a good rule of thumb that can be applied to all charities. We should expect them to use at least 65 percent of our contribution for the program activities. No more than 35 percent should be used for fund raising.

Questions To Stimulate Conversation

How do you decide which charities you want to support?

Should members with no recordable gift be permitted to serve on the governing board of the parish?

Do you know if your parish has a 52 Club? Should they be allowed to serve on the governing board?

Is your parish completely transparent about the money it receives and how it is expended?

CHAPTER THIRTEEN

Can Thankful Living Lead To Thankful Giving?

"Remember the Lord your God for it is God that gives you the ability to produce wealth (Deuteronomy 8:18)."

When my children were small one of their common complaints was *it's not fair*. They often compared themselves to some instance of good fortune being enjoyed by one of their siblings or friends. Occasionally, their tearful outcry against the universe was the result of a sporting contest or parental discipline. In our moments of self-revelation, we all have to admit that we too suffer such moments of outrage. *Life is not fair.*

We lose loved ones. Loved ones betray us. There are heartaches and heartbreaks. There is sickness, disease, and disability. Jobs are lost and marriages dissolve. Life is not easy, even for the best of us. Life is not perfect.

One of the toughest lessons to learn in life is that life will not be fair. There will be days when it appears that the bad guys are winning. There will be those moments when we feel like the guys in the white hats are getting the short end of the stick. Rare is the individual that hasn't learned the truth in the expression: *no good deed goes unpunished*. Sometimes, the less competent do get promoted over us. Occasionally, the slothful co-worker does get the recognition and the bonus. And, there are days that it appears that the good die young while troublemakers live on.

The story is told of Saint Teresa riding her donkey across the desert on a mission of mercy. In the middle of the desert, her donkey suddenly fell over and died. In the process, the donkey falls on her only water bag and smashes it. There she is in the middle of the desert with no donkey and no water. The legend is that at this point Saint Teresa shakes her fists at the heavens and shouts, "If this is the way you treat your friends, it is no wonder you have so few of them."

Comedian Robert Orben has a great line. "Sometimes I get the feeling that the whole world is against me. But then I regain my perspective and realize that some of the smaller nations are neutral on the subject."

Morris was faithful to the temple. Each Friday evening in his temple prayers, he would complain against God. "Why won't you let me win the lottery? It's not fair!" He would complain at great length. "You know that I'm a good husband. I'm a good father. I never miss temple. I say my prayers. If you would let me win the lottery I would give you a double tithe."

Day by day his complaints would continue. "Why do you hate me, God? Why am I not one of your favored ones? It is not fair. Answer me, why won't you let me win the lottery? My car is ten years old. I live in a tiny apartment. I want to winter in Florida. It gets so cold here when the snow falls."

Then one night in the midst of his complaints, he was interrupted by a great voice from heaven. "Morris, give me a break. Buy a ticket!"

I heard the story of a woman by the name of Helen Baker who had spent the majority of her life suffering with a rare nerve disorder. Yet every day she gives thanks to God for the chance to witness to others through her illness. She gives thanks to God for the strength she has gained from her troubles.

Gratitude is the fuel that energizes the soul.

When confronted with the injustices and the inconsistencies in the world, we are given two choices. The first is to complain against God. We can shout that it is not fair. Our second choice is to be grateful. This is the most difficult thing to do, yet gratitude is the fuel that energizes the soul.

In 1993, Robert Greene was severely injured in a traffic accident. He spent weeks in a coma. He spent a year in the hospital going through rehabilitation. In the middle of this grueling time, he wrote his mother a letter listing ten reasons he had to be thankful. His third reason was, "I have good strength in my arms to roll my wheelchair. Soon I will be able to walk on crutches." Reason number six, "Everything I have experienced has been of value to me." And reason number ten, "I am thankful I have a future that holds promise and opportunity."

He is thankful that he can get around in a wheelchair? He's thankful for months of painful rehabilitation? What kind of nut is this? Doesn't he understand that he should be complaining against God? This is not fair! Life is not fair! Instead, he's making out lists of reasons he has to be thankful.

How do we explain the difference? Two people suffering with two identical situations in life. The one becomes bitter, negative and filled with complaints. The second uses the experience to develop a positive, inspiring spirit. They are filled with a gratitude that becomes contagious.

Dorothy Soelle was a well-known professor of theology. She taught that there are two types of martyrs. If the pain and suffering we experience in this life makes us bitter, resentful, and hardens our hearts, then we become martyrs for the devil. If our suffering in this life makes us stronger, more compassionate, more understanding, more loving, then we become martyrs for God.

There is a Jewish tradition that insists that when we die, we will be held accountable on the Day of Judgment for all the blessings in this life for which we failed to be thankful.

In this tradition, there is a rabbinical story about a man who died and stood before the judgment seat of God. Immediately, he began complaining against the Almighty. "Remember when I was a small boy I told you all the things that I wanted in life?"

The Almighty responded, "Yes, it was a lovely dream."

"Then why did you not give me those things?" The man whined.

God replied, "I could have given you what you wanted, but I wanted to surprise you. I wanted to give you some things that were not a part of your dreams."

The man continued his complaints, "I wanted to be a scientist."

"I gave you the gifts to make you a very successful salesman."

The man shouted, "I wanted to be rich and famous."

"And I gave you a comfortable home, a faithful wife, nice friends."

He continued his list of grievances; "I wanted three sons."

118

God patiently smiled, "And I gave you three lovely daughters who are absolutely devoted to you."

The man's ingratitude could not be quashed. "I wanted you to give me what I wanted!"

And with all the love of the universe God patiently responded, "And I wanted you to want what I gave you."

The Talmud teaches, "Who is rich? The one who rejoices in what they already have."

In the face of the unfairness of life we choose just how we are going to respond. We can complain against God. In so doing, we will drown in a dark sea of bitterness and negativity. Or we can choose to trust in the transcendent goodness of God. If we do, our hearts will overflow with thankfulness and our souls will sing songs of gratitude.

An anonymous writer is credited with the following:

*If you woke up this morning and were able to hear the birds sing, use your vocal chords to utter human sounds, walk to the breakfast table on two good legs, and read the newspaper with two good eyes... you are more blessed than millions of those who could not do these things.

*If you have never experienced the danger of battle, the agony of torture, the loneliness of imprisonment, or the pangs of starvation... you are ahead of 500 million people in the world.

*If you can attend a church meeting without fear of harassment, arrest, torture, or death... you are more blessed than three billion people in the world.

*If you have food in the refrigerator, clothes on your back, a roof over your head, and a place to sleep... you are richer than 75 percent of this world.

*If you own your own computer, you are a select part of the 1% in the world who have one.

*If you have money in the bank, in your wallet, and spare change in a dish some place... you are among the top 8 percent of the wealthy in the world.

*If you are over thirty and either of your parents is still alive, you are very rare... over a billion people are orphans by the time they turn thirty.

*If you woke up this morning and are without pain and you enjoy more health than illness... you are more blessed than the many who will not even survive this day.

*If you hold up your head with a smile on your face and are truly thankful... you are blessed because the majority can, but most do not.

Who is rich?
The one that rejoices in what they already have.

I have seen a lot of strange epitaphs inscribed on cemetery headstones. I believe Charlie Mechem had written one of the best. He was head of Taft Broadcasting. Before he died, he instructed that the following be inscribed on his headstone.

Dear God,
Thanks for letting me visit this little planet in your vast universe. I had a wonderful time.

I have lived among the poorest of the poor on earth. I find it interesting that those who live in lands of scarcity worship a *God of Abundance*. Out of their poverty they open their hands to one another and respond with generosity. Yet, I find that too often those of us who live in a land of abundance worship a *God of Scarcity*. Our hands are constantly grabbing for more and our fists squeezing ever so tightly around that which we already have. In the face of our wealth, we profess poverty.

One of my favorite stories about Mother Teresa surrounds a visit by a group of tourists to one of her hospices in Calcutta. As they were being shown about the hospice, the group happened upon a patient that had vomited all over himself and onto the floor. There, kneeling among the stench and human vile, was one of Mother Teresa's nuns. She was quietly cleaning up the man and the vomit.

A tourist was heard to say, "Sister, I wouldn't do that for a million dollars."

The nun looked up and replied, "Sir, neither would I."

A grateful heart is a generous heart.
Count your blessings and not your burdens.

There just may be a limited number of things we are willing to do for money. Those things certainly define a portion of who we are. Those things we are willing to do that have no price tag, however, define our essence. Those things that money cannot buy define the substance of our being. We must know what those things are before we can know who we truly are. Those things in our life that we have valued and that are beyond price reflect the image of who we are.

As long as we define ourselves by the success symbols of this world, we will never have enough money. Any amount we do choose to share with Church or charity will be but a token by comparison. Generous giving begins when we are able to open our hearts in gratitude to the Almighty for the privilege of having visited this little planet in His vast universe.

Jim and Barbara were a young couple in my parish. They had been married for eight years and had a three-year old son. Jim was diagnosed with terminal bone cancer. He spent a great deal of time in the hospital. I had many opportunities to visit him. Frequently the visits were dark. Most were filled with Jim's tears, anger, fears, and the question. *Why is this happening to me?*

One afternoon I entered the hospital room to discover a bright smile on Jim's face. His entire countenance had changed. Our visit had a totally different tone. He talked about the many happy times in his life. He reflected on the love he had shared with his wife and son. As I was leaving, he asked me to give Barbara a message. He said, "Please tell her that I have finally figured it all out. Tell her that I now know where the party is located." He assured me she would know what he meant.

I returned to my office. About an hour later I got a telephone call advising me that

Jim had died. I immediately drove to their home so I could be with Barbara and their son. Barbara told me that, according to the floor nurse, I was the last person to talk to Jim. This gave me the opportunity to share with her the message Jim had given me. I told her what Jim had said.

Through tears she smiled and nodded, "As long as I've known Jim he has always compared himself to other people. He was convinced that everyone he knew was getting a better deal in life than he was. I told him on numerous occasions that he sounded just like a little boy that had not been invited to the popular kid's party. Thank God he finally figured it out. The party was inside him all the time."

Thankful living leads to thankful giving. Our checkbooks will open in thanksgiving to Church and charity when we discover the party that is the gift of life is inside each of us.

The Talmud asks, "Who is rich? The one who rejoices in what he already has."

Questions To Stimulate Conversation

Two people are faced with identical tragedies. The one becomes bitter while the other becomes a positive inspiration. How do you explain the difference?

How do you feel when you are in the presence of a person who is constantly complaining? How do you feel when you hear yourself complain?

What happens to your spirit when you are in the presence of a person filled with gratitude? How do you feel when you hear yourself give thanks?

How would your life be different if you could be thankful each day for that which you already have?

The author's thesis in this chapter is *thankful living leads to thankful giving.* Is he correct? Why or why not?

ABOUT THE AUTHOR

The Reverend Doctor Dennis R. Maynard is the author of sixteen books. Well over 200,000 Episcopalians have read his book, *Those Episkopols.* 3,500 congregations throughout the United States utilize *Those Episkopols* in their new member ministries. Several denominational leaders have called it the unofficial handbook for the Episcopal Church. He is also the author of *Forgive and Get Your Life Back.* That particular book has been used by the same number of clergy to do forgiveness training with the members of their congregations.

Maynard has written a series of novels focusing on life in the typical congregation. The nine books in this series of novels have received popular acceptance from both clergy and lay people. Readers anxiously await each new chapter in *The Magnolia Series*.

"The novels give us a chance to look at the underside of parish life. While the story lines are fictional, the readers invariably think they recognize the characters. If not, they know someone just like the folks that attend First Episcopal Church in the town of Falls City, Georgia."

His book, *When Sheep Attack,* is based on twenty-five case studies of clergy that were attacked by a small group of misguided antagonists in their congregations. These antagonists successfully removed their senior pastor, leaving the congregations divided and crippled. The book describes how it happened, what could have been done to stop it, and what can be done to prevent it from happening to your pastor and parish.

He has since written two additional books on the subject that have rapidly become best sellers. *Preventing A Sheep Attack* is being used to guide boards to establish mechanisms to prevent an attack. *Healing For Pastors and People Following A Sheep Attack* has brought comfort and healing to hundreds that have endured that nightmare. Faculty in theological schools in America, Canada, and several other countries use these three books as resource materials in their classes.

Doctor Maynard served some of the largest congregations in the Episcopal Church in America. His ministry included parishes in Illinois, Oklahoma, South Carolina, Texas, and California. President George H.W. Bush and his family are faithful members of the congregation he served in Houston, Texas. It is the largest congregation in the Episcopal Church.

He has served other notable leaders that represent the diversity of his ministry. These national leaders include Secretary of State, James Baker; Former Secretary of

Education, Richard Riley; Supreme Court Nominee, Clement Haynsworth; and the infamous baby doctor, Benjamin Spock, among others.

Doctor Maynard maintains an extensive travel schedule. He is frequently called on to speak, lead retreats, or serve as a consultant with parishes, schools, dioceses, and religious organizations throughout the United States and Canada.

He was ordained a priest at the age of twenty-four. His first assignments were as the curate at Grace Church and vicar of Saint Philip's Mission in Muskogee, Oklahoma. The bishop of the diocese charged him with closing Saint Philip's, an African-American congregation. He was to merge it with Grace Church. At the close of his first year the merger was realized.

He received a call to be vicar of Saint Mark's Mission in Dallas, Texas. In less than a year, the mission achieved parish status. The next year, he successfully led the merger of that parish with nearby Saint Margaret's Parish in Richardson, Texas. The combined congregations chose the name Church of the Epiphany. Over the next eight years they grew to a parish averaging one thousand people in attendance at five Sunday services, including a service in Mandarin.

Under his leadership, the congregation conducted three capital campaigns. One campaign was held to build a new church with a pipe organ, another to remodel the old nave into a parish hall, and one to build a parish life center.

The congregation started a counseling center, a bookstore, and a pre-school. It also became one of the centers for a teen drug abuse program and built a block partnership with an African-American Congregation in South Dallas.

The Epiphany congregation brought two large Vietnamese Refugee Families to Dallas, and helped them begin new and productive lives.

The parish was recognized for its growth and ministry in a 1978 article in *The Episcopalian,* the national newspaper for The Episcopal Church.

At the age of thirty-four, Maynard was called to historic Christ Church and School in Greenville, South Carolina. At the time, it was the seventh largest congregation in The Episcopal Church. Under his leadership, it grew to be the fourth largest with six Sunday services.

During his tenure the congregation set up four not for profit corporations. Each one administered a Food Bank, a soup kitchen, a free medical clinic, and a house for homeless men living with HIV and AIDS. The parish also built four Habitat For Humanity Houses while he was rector. Along with the diocese, the people of Christ Church worked with the Bishop of Haiti on several projects to meet the needs of the people of that diocese. The parish also established a bookstore, a pre-school, and a counseling center under his leadership.

At the time that Maynard went to Greenville, Christ Church Episcopal School was in decline. The school was being heavily subsidized by the parish budget. This was negatively impacting the growth and ministry programs in the congregation. Conversations were held among the leadership about closing the high school. There were more students withdrawing from the high school than were enrolling in it. Maynard and the head of school at the time began an aggressive student recruitment program and marketing campaign. Together they established a board of visitors and an annual fund for the school. After five years, the decline was reversed and the school began to grow.

Maynard led two capital campaigns to expand and improve the facilities for the parish and school at the downtown campus and broke ground for a new middle school building. The campaigns allowed for the renovation and expansion of the downtown campus property. The diocese had made the decision to close one of the mission churches in Greenville. He asked the bishop to make it a chapel of the parish to see if it couldn't be turned around. Saint Andrew's congregation became a self-supporting parish in just three years.

Maynard left Christ Church to become the Vice Rector of the largest congregation in The Episcopal Church, Saint Martin's in Houston, Texas. While there he was able to establish The Seabury Institute Southwest as a regional campus for Seabury Theological School in Chicago. Clergy were able to study and earn advanced degrees in congregational development through the institute.

Three years later the bishop and calling committee of Saint James by the Sea Parish in La Jolla, California approached him about becoming their rector. The bishop and vestry at the time were particularly concerned about the declining attendance and finances of the parish.

The parish was bleeding its endowment for daily operations and was quite literally living from bequest to bequest. Doctor Maynard believed himself called to be their rector. He was instrumental in discovering and convicting a long-time employee of the parish that had been embezzling large sums of money. He worked with the vestry leaders to establish internal controls and audits designed to prevent a reoccurrence. They established a separate board to safeguard the endowment of the parish. The pledge budget tripled in just three years. During his tenure, the parish also built up an operating reserve to meet projected obligations.

The congregation experienced rapid growth, often filling the four Sunday services. A very successful bookstore and gift shop was established. He led a capital campaign to address the deferred maintenance issues. The plan included provisions for making the property accessible to persons living with physical disabilities. The turnaround at St. James by the Sea was featured in an article in an international Anglican Magazine.

After four decades of parish ministry, Doctor Maynard retired in 2005 to pursue his growing consulting and writing ministry with the larger Church. Since his retirement he has worked with the bishops, clergy, schools, and congregations of thirty-one dioceses in the United States and Canada. He has become a best selling author of sixteen books. Several of his books are being used extensively in the congregations and schools of all denominations in the United States, Canada, England, and around the world.

Doctor Maynard's ministry has included service on several diocesan boards and committees. These included various diocesan program committees, director of summer camps for boys, diocesan trustee, finance committees, and executive committees. He was elected as the Regional Dean of various diocesan deaneries on several occasions. He was on the Cursillo secretariat and was spiritual director for the Cursillo Movement multiple times. Maynard served as co-chair for two diocesan capital campaigns.

In the National Episcopal Church, he served multiple terms on the board of the National Association of Episcopal Schools and as a trustee for Seabury Western Theological Seminary. He was appointed as an adjunct professor in congregational development at Seabury. Maynard was the co-coordinator for two national conferences designed for large congregations with multiple staff ministries.

Doctor Maynard was twice named to "*Oxford's Who's Who The Elite Registry of Extraordinary Professionals*" and to "*Who's Who Among Outstanding Americans.*"

Maynard completed two undergraduate degrees. He was awarded an Associate of Arts Degree in psychology and chemistry. His Bachelor of Arts Degree is a divisional major in the social sciences with a minor in biology. He completed a Masters Degree in theology. He earned a Doctor of Ministry Degree from Seabury Western Seminary in Congregational Development.

He currently resides in Rancho Mirage, California with his wife, Nancy Anne.

BOOKS BY
DENNIS R. MAYNARD

THOSE EPISKOPOLS
This is a popular resource for clergy to use in their new member ministries. It seeks to answer the questions most often asked about the Episcopal Church. Questions like: "Can You Get Saved in the Episcopal Church?" "Why Do Episcopalians Reject Biblical Fundamentalism?" "Does God Like All That Ritual?" "Are There Any Episcopalians in Heaven?" And others.

FORGIVEN, HEALED AND RESTORED
This book makes a distinction between forgiving those who have injured us and making the decision to reconcile with them or restore them to their former place in our lives.

THE MONEY BOOK
The primary goal of this book is to present some practical teachings on money and Christian Stewardship. It also encourages the reader not to confuse their self-worth with their net worth.

FORGIVE AND GET YOUR LIFE BACK
This book teaches the forgiveness process to the reader. It's a popular resource for clergy and counselors to use to do forgiveness training. In this book, a clear distinction is made between forgiving, reconciling, and restoring the penitent person to their former position in our lives.

WHEN SHEEP ATTACK

Your rector is bullied, emotionally abused, and then his ministry is ended. Your parish is left divided. Many faithful members no longer attend. This book is based on the case studies of twenty-five clergy who had just such an experience. What could have been done? What can you do to keep it from happening to you and your parish? Discussion questions are included that make it suitable for study groups.

PREVENTING A SHEEP ATTACK

This is a book that clergy and lay leaders can use to train and educate their leadership on ways to prevent a sheep attack. It explains why allowing a sheep attack to occur means that it is inevitable that someone will be ejected from the congregational system. He explains why parish and denominational leaders must choose.

HEALING FOR PASTORS & PEOPLE AFTER A SHEEP ATTACK

If you are a wounded senior minister, music minister, minister of education, or faithful lay leader that still suffers with the pain inflicted on you by a handful of antagonists, this book will assist you with your healing. Years later if you still wake in a cold sweat shaking from a nightmare filled with abusive memories, this book can help you. If you feel empty spiritually and unappreciated by the very Church you felt called to serve, this book will comfort you.

THE MAGNOLIA SERIES

BEHIND THE MAGNOLIA TREE (BOOK ONE)
Meet The Reverend Steele Austin. He is a young Episcopal priest who receives an unlikely call to one of the most prestigious congregations in the Southern United States. Soon his idealism conflicts with the secrets of sex, greed, and power at historic First Church. His efforts to minister to those living with AIDS and HIV bring him face to face with members of the Klu Klux Klan. Then one of the leading members seeks his assistance in coming to terms with the double life he's been living. The ongoing conflict with the bigotry and prejudice that are in the historic fabric of the community turn this book into a real page-turner.

WHEN THE MAGNOLIA BLOOMS (BOOK TWO)
In this the second book in the Magnolia Series, Steele Austin finds himself in the middle of a murder investigation. In the process, the infidelity of one of his closest priest friends is uncovered. When he brings an African-American priest on the staff, those antagonistic to his ministry find even more creative methods to rid themselves of the young idealist. Then a most interesting turn of events changes the African priest's standing in the parish. A young associate undermines the rector by preaching a gospel of hate, alienating most of the women in the congregation and all the gay and lesbian members. The book closes with a cliffhanger that will leave the reader wanting another visit to Falls City, Georgia.

PRUNING THE MAGNOLIA (BOOK THREE)

Steele Austin's vulnerability increases even further when he uncovers a scandal that will shake First Church to its very foundation. In order to expose the criminal, he must first prove his own innocence. This will require him to challenge his very own bishop. The sexual sins of the wives of one of the parish leaders present a most unlikely pastoral opportunity for the rector. In the face of the ongoing attacks of his antagonists, Father Steele Austin is given the opportunity to leave First Church for a thriving parish in Texas.

THE PINK MAGNOLIA (BOOK FOUR)

The Rector's efforts to meet the needs of gay teenagers that have been rejected by their own families cast a dark cloud over First Church. A pastoral crisis with an antagonist transforms their relationship from enemies to friends. The Vestry agrees to allow the Rector to sell the church-owned house and purchase his own, but not all in the congregation approve. The reader is given yet another view of church politics. This particular book ends with the most suspense-filled cliffhanger yet.

THE SWEET SMELL OF MAGNOLIA (BOOK FIVE)

The fifth book in the Magnolia Series follows the Rector's struggle with trust and betrayal in his own marriage. His suspicions about his wife take a heavy toll on his health and his ministry. He brings a woman priest on the staff in face of the congregation's *objections to doing so. Some reject her ministry totally. Then the internal politics of the Church are exposed even further with the election of a Bishop. Those with their own agenda manipulate the election itself. Just when you think the tactics of those opposed to the ministry of Steele Austin can't go any lower, they do.*

THE MAGNOLIA AT SUNRISE (BOOK SIX)
The lives of The Reverend Steele Austin and the people of First Church face new challenges. Father Austin takes his sabbatical time to examine his life's purpose. Still stinging from the most recent attacks on his wife and himself from the antagonists in his congregation, he wrestles with the decision as to whether or not he wants to return to First Church. He is even uncertain if he wants to remain in the priesthood.

THE CHANGING MAGNOLIA (BOOK SEVEN)
The masters of the great plantations ruled over those they believed to be inferior to them. Their descendants often believe they are entitled to this same position. With divine right, they appeal to their wealth and bloodline, demanding that the less important in their world be subservient to them. In Falls City, Georgia, those holding positions of superiority utilize intimidation, slander, blackmail, sex, and even murder to get their way. In this seventh visit to Historic First Church, these powerful people have used their influence to destroy the spirit of their own pastor and his family.

THE MAGNOLIA AT CHRISTMAS (BOOK EIGHT

All the characters that the readers have loved return to Falls City and First Church for Christmas. Their holiday celebration will bring a smile to your face, an occasional chuckle, and most certainly a tear. Christmas is a happy time in Falls City. You'll want to celebrate it at First Church. It ends with one of the biggest shocks and surprises yet. Readers are now anxiously awaiting Book Nine to be released the autumn of 2017.

All of Doctor Maynard's books can be viewed and ordered on his website.
www.Episkopols.com

Discounts on most of his books are available through his website.

Visit Amazon.com to discover Doctor Maynard's books that are on Kindle.

WWW.EPISKOPOLS.COM

78976188R10078

Made in the USA
Columbia, SC
23 October 2017